ORPHANS OF THE LIVING

A Study of Bastardy

BY THE SAME AUTHOR
Backward Christian Soldiers

DIANA DEWAR

Orphans of the Living
A Study of Bastardy

HUTCHINSON OF LONDON

HUTCHINSON & CO (*Publishers*) LTD
178–202 Great Portland Street, London W1

London Melbourne Sydney
Auckland Bombay Toronto
Johannesburg New York

*

First published 1968

This book has been set in Times Roman, printed in Great Britain
on Antique Wove paper by The Camelot Press Ltd., London and Southampton,
and bound by Wm. Brendon, Tiptree, Essex
09   089120   1

Contents

For
My Mother

Introduction

THIS book is about the greatest human grief apart from death: lost love and forlorn children, children in mourning for phantom parents. Death is the ultimate brutality for the bereaved because it is final, but orphans secure in past love might be regarded as fortunate compared with illegitimate and abandoned children for whom separation is a continuing desolation of life.

The plight of a solitary deserted child in an institution would arouse spontaneous responses and bring warm-hearted offers to give the child the love of a real home. When there is a group of children in an institution of any kind their very number anaesthetizes emotion and their problems cease to be individually human and urgent, becoming instead primarily a matter of administration. The emptiness of their separate plights becomes obscured and institutional welfare takes over, effectively insulating the conscience of those moved to help from personal involvement. The good-intentioned can now join a committee and help the institution to run efficiently: the fund of pity which might have removed the need for the Home has been subtly channelled towards its permanence.

It is not true of children to say that trouble shared is trouble diminished. This is the appearance present-day institutions offer. The reality is a large number of human tragedies, made the more piteous because the victims are too young to comfort each other and often not old enough to have understood the separation that has bereft them of parental love.

True, in an institution all immediate and obvious needs of the children are catered for: they have everything, yet nothing worth having because living without the embrace of love is pointless to children and old people, indeed to most of us.

Twenty children in an institution (and twenty is a modest number) do not seem the same outrage as one child's misery, their personal and unique tragedies appear acceptable because they are shared within a tidy and clinical solution.

The majority of children in long-term institutional care are illegitimate. Illegitimacy in Britain today remains a sin with its own social penalties victimizing the babies, punishing the mothers and undermining the happiness and stability of rising generations. The dilemma of society today is that while it does not wish to ostracize the children it is not prepared to accept the mothers. People will give generously to children's charities and are kind-hearted in helping children's homes, but many still nurse moral prejudices about helping unmarried mothers. They are reluctant to concede that the best way to help the child is to help his mother and that her motherhood is inviolable.

In 1966 there were 67,056 illegitimate babies born in England and Wales, one in thirteen of all births. In Greater London one in every nine babies was illegitimate and in some boroughs the figure rose to one in five. The national figures for illegitimate births are the highest for a generation and are still rising, particularly in the twenty to twenty-four age group. In 1966 over a thousand babies were born to girls under sixteen, and the total of 20,582 illegitimate children born to mothers under twenty is more than twice that of 1960. It might be assumed that because illegitimacy is so widely prevalent today it has become more acceptable; that the growing population of illegitimate children has brought new tolerance. This is not the case. The taboos of the past have deep roots, and the traditional belief that illegitimate children are of inferior worth lingers on, sometimes consciously but more often perhaps as an unconscious condemnation. Maybe this archaic and shameful prejudice is rooted in a fear of our own sexuality and a desire to punish others for behaviour that we forbid ourselves. Whatever the reason the very expression 'illegitimate child' is an offence against charity: all children must be equally deserving of love and their birthright should be the security of being wanted.

It is on the paternalistic pretext of marking approval and support of marriage that legal and social systems have for centuries attached disabilities to illegitimate children. In the Middle Ages a child born illegitimately was a *filius nullius*, a child of no one. Today the child born out of wedlock has progressed from being a legally unknown parentless person to a child with a mother who has some rights and duties towards him. But he remains as legally fatherless as ever he was. The shortened form of birth certificate excluding reference to parentage was not introduced until ¡1953. Until 1964 an illegitimate person could not be ordained a priest without special dispensation. Bastards still cannot inherit titles or entailed property, join the Metropolitan Police, and by tradition may be refused admission to one of the biggest clubs in Britain, Freemasonry.

These disabilities reveal how deep-sown attitudes are slow to change.

But perhaps the most destructive of all handicaps for the illegitimate child are his own innate feelings of inferiority, of being unwanted, denied a known ancestry and a family history or mythology. He finds it more difficult to realize his own personality because of this sharp severance from the past, and may feel guilt at his very existence, perhaps taking upon himself some of the guilt that his mother feels. For all unmarried mothers do feel guilt in greater or lesser degree despite a frequent façade of shamelessness. They receive small sympathy from the public, however, because they have transgressed the golden rule of expediency—never be caught—which is the basis of common morality.

The National Council for the Unmarried Mother and Her Child has considerable influence as a reformist agency in legal and social spheres, and is respected as a practical fount of uncensorious help. But it remains an unpopular charity because there persists this prejudice that those who help unmarried mothers countenance profligacy. Mrs. Margaret Bramall, the general secretary, says that nearly everywhere she speaks some well-intentioned person will get up and ask in apparent sincerity: 'If we help the mother are we not encouraging immorality?'

A woman wrote to the National Council for the Unmarried Mother and Her Child after a television appeal in 1966: 'I wouldn't waste a penny on them . . . we all know why they do it—to trap a husband.' This letter was typical of many, revealing an antique repository of ignorance, intolerance, and feelings of vengeance.

Flagsellers for moral welfare work also meet these attitudes at the front door, while those collecting for Dr. Barnardo's are never challenged about the rectitude of their cause.

Those who resent help for unmarried mothers may be accused of many things—ignorance, sanctimony, poverty of imagination, small concern over great suffering—but principally they must be indicted for showing an obsessive indignation with the unwed mothers while shirking the fact that the welfare of the mothers is inextricably bound up with the fate of the guiltless children. What happens to the children?

In this country less than 25 per cent of illegitimate children are adopted, but the percentage of those unmarried mothers who fail in their intention to keep their babies is not known. It is certain there are many without the support of their families who find they cannot make a home for themselves and their children because financial pressures and social strictures are too great for them. The Home Office analysis of causes why children come into the care of local authorities gives as the reason for 3,062 admissions in the year 1966–7 'child illegitimate, mother unable to provide', and illegitimate children remain the hard core of children in long-term care. Social agencies are also concerned at the number of mothers who capitulate to the realities of their situation and surrender older babies for adoption.

Illegitimacy is probably the biggest single cause of unhappy children today because bastardy remains so widely socially unacceptable.

But there are many other reasons for which children may need public care, and these children should be on our consciences too because public caring is a poor substitute for individual caring. The Children's Act of 1948 laid a duty on local authorities to provide for children deprived of normal care and this may have been the worst thing it did. It appeared to exonerate the community from ordinary neighbourliness and kindness, and to condone those half-hearted relatives and friends who are less inclined or able to look after the children of a sick mother now that it is generally regarded as the duty of the Children's Officer to do so. Home Office figures show that the number of children in the care of local authorities in England and Wales in 1966-7 was 69,405 and that the turnover was rapid, 53,381 being admitted and 53,187 discharged during the year. About 80 per cent of the children who went out of care were restored to parents or friends. Only 284 of the children taken into care were without parent or guardian. More than half were admitted because of the illness of a parent or because the mother was having a baby. Some were deserted by their mother and the father was unable to look after them. Others were there because a parent was in prison. Homeless families and unsatisfactory home conditions were other causes. In the same year, 4,599 children were committed into the care of local councils by court orders. These orders nominate a local authority as a 'fit person' and give to the council the same rights and duties as the parents—but with prior claims of possession. Less than a third of the orders made concerned children who had committed any offence, but children who are subjects of 'fit person' orders comprise another large group in long-term care. In 1967 they numbered over 22,000.

In addition to the State's army of children in care, there are another 9,863 being looked after by voluntary organizations. So, in 1967, a total of 79,268 children were cared for away from their parents, and however inadequate parental love and care may appear, it is something irreplaceable for the young child.

There is widespread agreement now that children do not develop to the best of their potentiality without a secure family background and that communal care among strangers is an insensitive way to look after them. The public care of these children in 1966-7 cost more than thirty-two and a half million pounds, and voluntary care another five or six millions.

Even if we cannot create a community caring enough to save many of these children from institutionalization and much of the money this costs, there are powerful arguments to suggest that many millions of pounds could be more effectually, and more charitably, invested in forms of direct help to keep the family, however incomplete, together.

It is true that since the Children's Act of 1948 local authorities have been under an obligation to find foster homes for children in their care whenever possible, and half the children they look after are now boarded out. When the Children's Act was passed less than 35 per cent of children in public care were in foster homes. Now the national average is 50 per cent, but there are wide variations from over 90 per cent in some areas to under 20 per cent in others. Voluntary organizations also board out, some more widely than others; but only about one-seventh of all the children in their charge are cared for this way.

What is also sadly true is that foster homes often fail and the children have to be removed. Accurate figures are difficult to obtain—no one likes admitting failure—but it has been estimated that between a third and two-fifths of long-term foster homes fail in their purpose. Children who have known institutional care in infancy frequently fail to settle in foster homes. One of the chief reasons is that they are unable to respond demonstratively and quickly to the affection shown them. It takes a rare saintliness to continue to shower love upon a child when any reciprocation is painfully slow to show itself.

It is not unusual for some children committed into the care of local authorities to know as many as ten different homes in five years. A government-sponsored inquiry into the destinies of children in three different areas who were committed into the care of the local authorities by the juvenile courts in 1945, 1950, and 1955, showed that the frequency with which children were moved from foster homes has doubled in ten years. On average in 1955 children boarded out were moved once a year. Foster parents either asked for the child's removal or the authorities deemed it desirable. Ironically, one reason for this tragically worsening situation is an enlightened change of policy which puts greater emphasis on rehabilitating the family.

Children in care see much more of their parents. Before the 1948 Children's Act children committed to care were often taken away from their parents completely and placed in permanent foster homes. Now, the foster home has become less permanent, good foster parents have become scarcer, for many find contact with the natural parents disturbing and dread a final parting with a child whom they hoped to make one of the family. While this new policy of striving to keep the child in close touch with his own family appears praiseworthy, the effect upon the child may be traumatic. Impermanence is a complete denial of everything home stands for and everything for which a child yearns. There is evidence that in the worst cases changes of foster home are seen by the child as repeated rejection and make many children lonely and difficult, no longer trusting the world as a warm and loving place. The moves produce problem children, whose difficulties derive from inexpressible feelings of betrayal beyond their comprehension.

Another crucial factor in the failure of so many foster homes is the inadequate quality of the work permitted from child care officers. The child care officer is badly underpaid and grossly overworked. He is also often ill-qualified or quite unqualified, although the casualties of any incompetence are children. In 1967, there were fifty-one children's departments with no trained staff at all and another thirty-five departments had 20 per cent and less.

Apart from institutional care and fostering, about 22,000 children a year are placed for adoption. There are sixty-five registered adoption societies in England and Wales and eighty-five local authorities also elect to carry out this work. These adoption agencies may be by-passed, for adoption can also be arranged by direct placement by the mother, or through a third party. The third party may be a well-meaning woman in the fish queue, a priest, a doctor, the matron of a nursing home, a lawyer, or just a mutual friend. In fact some 8,500 of the 22,000 adoptions a year are made through third-party arrangements and this alarms the professionals who maintain the third party thinks more about helping an unmarried mother or a childless couple than about the welfare of the baby.

Increasingly it is being proclaimed that responsible adoption requires casework of a high calibre, careful interviewing, and perception enhanced by training and experience if the happiness of the children is to be safeguarded.

But while there is constant effort to improve the methods of adoption societies, an important new factor has arisen. The supply and demand situation has changed radically; a few years ago there were ten times as many prospective adopters as children available; today the gap is narrowing and agencies find it more difficult to place children for adoption. In the new circumstances there might well develop a conflict between the intellectual wish for a greater sophistication in adoption procedures and the human need to be less selective.

It can well be argued that selection can become over-sophisticated. It is tempting to scrutinize the motives of prospective adopters too critically. It is not always easy to remember that there are good, bad, and indifferent parents, whether their children are their own or adopted. In the same way that no child can be labelled 'guaranteed for adoption', no adult can be underwritten as an adopter. At the heart of the problem, however, remains the simple truth that for the child almost any parents are better than none.

Dr. A. M. McWhinnie, former director of The Guild of Service, Edinburgh, in her research study with fifty-eight adults who had been adopted as children showed they had formed strong emotional ties with their adoptive parents and identified closely with them, irrespective of whether the adoption had been regarded as particularly happy or unhappy.

Many infants whose mothers are willing for them to be adopted cannot be found adopters. Thousands of these unwanted babies are coloured. There are no available figures, possibly because there is fear of exposing an unpalatable situation and inflaming colour prejudice. The Home Office told me: 'No information is available about the nationality or colour of children in care'. Dr. Barnardo's estimate a quarter of the children in their care are 'coloured', and the Church of England Children's Society calculate that the same proportion of their children are born of 'mixed races'.

Thousands more children are too often dismissed as unadoptable because they are mentally or physically handicapped, although they, above all children, need the love and encouragement of a real home and an accepting community. Their handicap, like the yoke of illegitimacy, also carries a stigma, and the fact that this is not often made explicit or even consciously realized in no way detracts from its potency. Attitudes towards deformity and infirmity are primitive and stem from ancient superstitions. They are, perhaps, the more powerful for that, and too often, even today, abnormal children are regarded as ominous portents or as punishments upon erring parents. Frequently the public concern for such children is directed towards the provision of special homes and schools. The solution is a tidy one which absolves the community from the pain of personal confrontation but it withholds from the children the balm of individual caring.

There are also the children who have not been adopted or fostered in infancy through administrative delays, or simply because there are too few child-care officers and all are over-worked. Sometimes it is the indecision and inadequacy of the children's natural mothers which robs them of love and security. There are mothers who cannot make a home for their children and yet will not allow others to do so. Other children may not have enjoyed a clean bill of health in infancy, often for minor reasons. They can grow rapidly from desirable, appealing babies to more demanding young children, often now with objectionable habits, more difficult to place and unreservedly to embrace.

The public conscience has been lulled on the fate of all these children. The common fallacies are: that there are far more prospective adopters than children available; that those who are not adopted remain with their own mothers, or in the modern Children's Homes which are model establishments of enlightenment; or better still, that the children will be looked after by devoted house parents in small Cottage Homes or Family Homes. On this last point it should be said that the Church of England Children's Society's family homes have at least fifteen children. On average there are thirteen children in Council Homes and twenty-eight in Voluntary Homes. Also there is great difficulty in finding the right staff, dedicated but well-balanced mature people who will stay.

It is my contention that in this country countless children in need still suffer from patronage without heart. Children's Homes are still rooted in a compromise between a social conscience which demands the professional implementation of ethical intentions towards unwanted anonymous children, and a widespread emotional frigidity which inhibits the will or the ability to give personal loving care.

This shallow concern derives its emotional anaemia from the impersonal ethic and the caring of children as a social duty. It provides for a public display of pity rather than demanding a personal expenditure of love and identification. Too often giving is related to the needs of the giver and not to the needs of the recipient. Too often the middle-aged committee woman needs an interest; the born organizer an outlet; the wealthy, gratitude for their largesse.

The children's needs are simpler yet more difficult to arrange. No amount of public or private charity can be compensation for vanished parents. But the enduring and exclusive love of an ordinary home is a good substitute and certainly preferable to the sad counterfeit of true family life provided by institutions.

I realize there are many entire books written on some of the chapters which form this book but I have not set out to write a definitive work. This is a polemic, an appeal, inspired by anger and distress. While experts equivocate, sociologists design research projects, and charities raise money, children are waiting in the wings. The very existence of children whom nobody wants is an uncomfortable cold truth. The existence of children who are very much wanted by their own mothers, but forsaken because their single parent cannot provide for them is also a painful reality which should stir the conscience and the heart.

There is a vast specialist literature on deprived children, and as can only be expected the experts are at variance on numberless points. But there is still a surprisingly large area of common agreement reached by the evidence from scientific research all over the world. One important question raised by this book is why this research is in the main unapplied? It is not enough for research to be carried out with diligent care and its results documented in the strange language of the discipline and read by other sociologists. Its findings must be taken into practical account and implemented without decades of delay, because children are perishable.

Another argument central to my case is that well-intentioned private charity, however enlightened and imaginative, does long-term harm by preventing the proper acceptance of responsibility needing action by the State and by us all. An unwanted child should not be a 'charity child' dependent on disinterested patronage, but a charge upon our common humanity.

I have tried in this book as a non-specialist, but a concerned parent, to present the hard facts, tried theories, and current controversies to other non-specialist but equally concerned men and women. It is an appeal for a more widely compassionate view of the problem; to offer the anonymity of impersonal shelter is not sufficient and we are all guilty in not building a community which cares enough. One child's tragedy grieves the heart, wounds the imagination. This tragedy multiplied prohibits the same identification. Its cruelty is concealed in an oblivion of numbers.

The curse of charity lies in its frequent assumption of superiority. Too often there persists the old-fashioned patronage which humiliates and chastizes as well as a fashionable charity which condescends. It is our privilege to succour mothers and children whatever their status, and our failure is their crucifixion and ours:

'But whoso shall offend one of these little ones which believe in me, it were better for him that a millstone were hanged about his neck, and that he were drowned in the depth of the sea.'

ST. MATTHEW 19:6

B

1

History

THERE is a strongly embedded British belief that effective social reform can be won only gradually over the centuries. To make haste slowly is the comfortable maxim that aims to woo public opinion to greater tolerance and liberalism whilst causing the least offence and disruption. Such diplomatic caution ignores the immediacy of the plight for those unfortunates concerned. Certainly the English laws governing illegitimacy, and the social attitudes evinced, have been oppressively slow to change, and this tardiness has meant immeasurable unhappiness to unprivileged generations.

Even the very brief review possible here of the shocking history of reforms concerning bastardy reveals a woeful tale of ignorance and bigotry relieved only by the visions and achievements of a few great men and women.

Both legislation concerning illegitimate children, and modes of thinking about them, still embody some harsh assumptions from the Middle Ages. Bastards were then *filii nullius*, children of no one, without rights, legal nonentities: their existence was an offence against not only God's law but man's law; and those who tried to help them were accused of condoning immorality and encouraging licentiousness.

The medieval idea was that an illegitimate child without legal family had no rights and nobody was beholden to him. He was the responsibility of the Poor Law authorities and often a charge upon the rates of the parish where he was born. Indeed, it was the determination of the parish officers to compel his begetters to pay for him that led to the recognition of a legal connection between the illegitimate child and the natural parents.

The first Bastardy Act (1576) says that the burden of caring for illegitimate children is 'defrauding of the relief of the impotent and aged true poor' of the parish, and 'an evil example and encouragement of the lewd life'. The Act ordered natural parents to pay for the upkeep of their offspring 'as well for the punishment of the mother and reputed father of such bastard child, as also the better relief of every such parish'. By the eighteenth century the practical basis of this piece of legislation found extension, for by then not only was the maintenance of the illegitimate child considered the joint responsibility of both parents, but a single woman could name the father. Unless he could prove his innocence, the 'father' was liable upon the mother's word alone to indemnify the parish for the cost of the child's support, or face the bleak alternative of the common gaol, or marry the woman. According to the Poor Law Commissioners, appointed in 1832 to investigate the conduct of the Poor Law, marriage in these circumstances was declared to be founded 'on fear on one side and vice on both'.

The Poor Law Commissioners in the early nineteenth century criticized the Bastardy laws because they allowed too easily for the punishment of innocent men if unmarried mothers were unscrupulously determined to name 'fathers'. More importantly, they felt that the just investigation of these accusations was overridden by concern to find men to assume the financial burden of the illegitimate and so relieve the local ratepayers. The Commissioners suggested remedies which reinforced the popular view of the day, that it was the woman with an illegitimate baby who was guilty of succumbing to temptation and the man was not to be equally blamed. The acceptance of this double standard of morality, which is still widely prevalent today, led to the Poor Law Amendment Act of 1834. This made it plain that unmarried mothers were responsible for their children. In future the unmarried mother was to be obliged to support the child and to provide his only inheritance, although if a child became a charge upon the rates the parish could still make a maintenance order against the putative father. This provision, however, was purely a sop to the ratepayers and an irrational one, for it meant that the mother's right to seek an affiliation order depended upon whether or not her child was a charge upon the parish. In effect, it had been decided that erring women should suffer to the full the consequences of a 'fall'.

Although the unmarried mother was made virtually the only legal provider, there was no recognition at this time of her claim to legal parenthood. She still had no rights or legal status for herself. In 1841 a court ruled that the mother of Ann Lloyd,[1] an illegitimate child, had no valid claim to her daughter's custody. Discussing the mother's action, one of the judges summed up the grounds for refusal in a rhetorical question: 'How does the mother of an illegitimate child differ from a stranger?'

Happily, more humanitarian views were gaining ascendancy over both religious bigotry and rhetoric, and these began to influence legislation. The Bastardy Act of 1845 enabled justices to make maintenance orders of up to half-a-crown a week against presumed fathers if the mothers could bring sufficient corroborative evidence.

Fortunately too, the Ann Lloyd case did not establish a precedent, and the courts began to hold that a mother had the legal right to regain her illegitimate child from persons to whom she had surrendered him. Today these basic rights of the mother over her child are entrenched by twentieth-century legislation, noticeably the Adoption Act of 1926 and its successors, which lay down that an illegitimate child may not be adopted without his mother's consent, unless it is decided she is withholding her agreement unreasonably. As a result, at long last, one legal parent has been secured for the innocently illegal child. But improvements in the legal status of the unmarried mother have not been equalled in the case of the unmarried father. The illegitimate child is still fatherless by law.

It is estimated that in this country about one man in twenty-five fathers an illegitimate child.[2] He does so with increasing rights over his children and diminishing responsibilities towards them. In fact, he has no obligations at all unless the mother resolutely exercises her own initiative. Apart from the affront to personal dignity and pride, it is not surprising when one considers the legal steps an unmarried mother must still take to obtain some redress from the baby's father, that only about 10 per cent of illegitimate children have fathers named in affiliation orders.[3]

The unmarried mother has to apply to the criminal court for proceedings against the presumed father, and she must normally do so before the child is a year old. (Exceptions are made if the man has gone abroad or if the case is brought by the Ministry of Social Security or the local authority.) She must offer sufficient evidence to justify the issue of a summons, and then, if her action succeeds, she may receive from the magistrates an affiliation order instructing the father to pay a regular sum towards the child's support. The maximum she might be awarded was raised from half-a-crown to five shillings in 1872,[4] to one pound in 1925,[5] to thirty shillings in 1952,[6] and to fifty shillings in 1960.[7] It should be emphasized that today fifty shillings a week is the most that can be legally demanded from the father; but, in fact, the average amount fixed by the magistrates is much smaller and, of course, the man may pay even less than the sum decided, or fail to pay at all. The mother has to apply for another summons for arrears of main-tenance or non-payment, and, once again, the courts act only upon her instigation.

The last decade, however, brought important legislation con-cerning the status of the illegitimate father. The significant changes began with the Adoption Act 1958 which for the first time recognized that the presumed father's views on his child's future should be heeded, and made provision for his intervention.

In adoption proceedings the court appoints an officer, usually a welfare worker, to act as the child's guardian *ad litem*. A putative father contributing under an affiliation order, or by agreement, to his child's support had long had the right to be notified of adoption proceedings, but the 1958 Act places the onus upon the Guardian *ad litem* 'to inform the court if he learns of any person, claiming to be the father, who wishes to be heard by the court on the question of whether an adoption order should be made'. How far the Guardian *ad litem* should actively seek to find the natural father is still not entirely clear; but the Act remains an important legislative landmark.

The next milestone is the Legitimacy Act 1959 which gave the unmarried father the right to apply to a court for custody and access, although it did not confer any pre-eminent rights upon the natural father. Misunderstandings over this last point has created some controversy about the intention of the 1959 Act and it has been asked whether this was not in conflict with the 1958 Adoption Act. The Legitimacy Act, however, did nothing to strengthen the position of the unmarried father in adoption cases: he was still unable to approve or veto the adoption of his natural child. It merely enabled him to apply for custody himself. His fatherhood would be considered when determining what course was best for the child's welfare. The weight the courts attach to the claims of the putative father depends not only upon circumstances, but the opinions of the justices themselves. In 1964 Lord Denning ruled 'the fatherhood was not an overriding consideration'.[8] Two years later the Court of Appeal heard what came to be known as the 'blood tie' case[9] in which there was a conflict of opinion between the judges. Two of the three Lords Justice (Lord Justice Harman and Lord Justice Russell) held that an instinctive bond existed between a natural parent and his child and that the infant would lose an important factor in the development of his personality if he were not brought up by his natural father. Lord Justice Willmer, who presided, disagreed. He said: 'At present the child has a settled home with the adopters, who love him, who have looked after him devotedly for seventeen months, and who have the means to give him a good education and good Christian upbringing. If the father is to have his way all this is to be sacrificed.' Lord Justice Willmer referred to evidence of a psychiatrist who had spoken of long-lasting or permanent impairment of a child's capacity to form any love-relationship, by a change of mother.

Clearly, the laws are interpreted variously. Nevertheless, the intention of recent legislation can be simply stated: the human needs of the child must take precedence when considering competing claims.

It is almost incredible that such simple wisdom should have taken so long to find expression in law, and yet reforms are often delayed for centuries by blinkered traditionalists and revengeful moralists. It was not until the Legitimacy Acts of 1926 and 1959 that the indelibility of bastardy in English law was changed. It took both these Acts to make it possible for illegitimate children to become legitimate through the subsequent marriage of their parents[10] although the reform had been proposed seven centuries earlier by the Church. The common law held that children illegitimately born could not be legitimized: the canon law of the Church maintained that children could be legitimized by the subsequent marriage of their parents. At the Council of Merton in 1234 the Bishops asked the Barons to change the English law of inheritance to allow a child born before the marriage of his parents to inherit his father's land at the father's death. The Barons refused in categorical terms: 'All the Earls and Barons replied with one voice that they would on no account change the laws of England as they had been observed and approved hitherto.'

Another limited reform brought in by the Legitimacy Act of 1926 gave an illegitimate person the right to succeed when the mother dies intestate and without any legitimate children. This is the exception to the rule that an illegitimate person has no right to share in the estate of either of his parents unless named as a beneficiary under a will, for it has long been a presumption of law that any gift to 'children', 'issue', and 'descendants' in anyone's will applies to legitimate relationship only.

This precise point was put to the test in October 1966[11] when the Court of Appeal by a majority ruled that an illegitimate girl of four could not share in her natural father's life insurance policy of five hundred pounds, although she had clearly been treated as her father's daughter during his lifetime.

Lord Denning, Master of the Rolls, said in a dissenting judgment: 'We should throw over these harsh rules of the past. They are not rules of law. They are only guides to the construction of documents and are quite out of date.'

The child was clearly 'related' and a 'descendant' of her father. 'When we say we are all descended from Adam and Eve we mean descended by blood, not by marriage.'

The Court was being pressed to give the words 'relation' and 'descendant' an extraordinary meaning—that in the eyes of the law the young girl was the daughter of nobody and related to no one:

that she was an outcast and was to be shut out from any part in her father's insurance benefit.

'No doubt that argument would have been accepted in the nineteenth century,' said Lord Denning. 'The judges in those days used to think that if they allowed illegitimate children to take benefit they were encouraging immorality. They laid down narrow, pedantic rules and in so doing acted in accordance with their contemporary morality. Even Victorian fathers did what they thought right when they turned their erring daughters out of the house. They visited the sins of the fathers upon the children with a vengeance.'

Disagreeing with Lord Denning's view that there should be a more rational approach today, Lord Justice Diplock said that in popular language 'descendants' was capable of including or excluding bastards. There was no decision on whether an illegitimate child was to be included under an insurance scheme, and so the Court might feel free to decide as it pleased. But this was a legal document, and it specifically provided that in the case of dispute it should be interpreted by a lawyer. So the words in it should be given, not their popular, but a legal meaning.

Lord Justice Russell, who also disagreed with Lord Denning, quoted the appeal of Bassanio in the 'Merchant of Venice':

'*And I beseech you,*
Wrest once the law to your authority:
To do a great right, do a little wrong.'

To which Portia replied:

'*It must not be. There is no power in Venice can alter a decree*
established:
'*Twill be regarded for a precedent,*
And many an error by the same example will rush into the state.
It cannot be.'

'I am a Portia man,' added Lord Justice Russell.

Lord Denning termed these 'nineteenth century attitudes': in fact they are feudal: an illegitimate child in the Middle Ages was 'a child of no one' without any legally recognized forebears, and the barest charity towards him was considered dangerously misguided.

When Thomas Coram, English sea-captain and philanthropist, opened Britain's first foundling hospital in London in the first half of the eighteenth century, he received a grant from public funds which was attacked on the grounds that it was likely to increase the evil it was seeking to cure: 'There will unhappily be too much Reason for saying that this present Humanity will be future cruelty'.[12]

There was no doubt about the appalling need for such an institution. Foundling hospitals had been established in France and Italy as early as the seventh and eighth centuries, and an earlier attempt to provide for abandoned children in this country was made by Christ's Hospital in 1552, but by the middle seventeenth century it had become reputable and would only accept legitimate children.[13]

Demands for admission to the Coram Foundling Hospital soon outstripped accommodation, and in 1756 Parliament granted the Hospital a subsidy of ten thousand pounds on condition that all children brought to their doors were admitted.

This system was alleged to have debased standards and led to abuse, so in 1761 admission became selective and took into account individual circumstances. Thomas Coram and his friends were businessmen as well as philanthropists and they extended the aims of their charity to provide the children in their care with training and apprenticeships which would help to safeguard their futures.

Many famous men of the period served the Hospital including Hogarth and Handel. Hogarth, who was a Governor, persuaded leading artists to give works of art to the Hospital for exhibition to the public. As the Hospital's collection grew so did the number of visitors and 'the Foundlings' became the fashionable morning lounge of the reign of George II—another example of the ironic way in which the charitable attracts the fashionable.

In the twentieth century the Coram Hospital moved into the country and for about twenty years it was situated at Berkhamsted in Hertfordshire. It was closed down in 1954, although its work for children continues on modern enlightened lines.

Today the name of the 'Foundling Hospital' is changed to 'The Thomas Coram Foundation for Children' and its work is centred in London. Unlike many ancient charities it has revised its policy to interpret and apply the widely humanitarian intentions of the founder to present-day circumstances. A contemporary venture is the fostering of illegitimate babies for mothers who cannot make up their minds about their future, or who cannot immediately have their babies with them. It provides excellent casework services and claims it has never had a failure in ten years of making fostering arrangements. As many as 60 per cent of the babies are reunited with their natural mothers within two years; but the Coram Foundation remains selective, and stipulates that a child accepted into their care must be the mother's only illegitimate baby.

One of the reasons which prompted Thomas Coram to found his charity was the appalling number of illegitimate children who died before they were one year old. Many unmarried mothers of the early eighteenth century were so ashamed and desperate that they left their babies to perish by the roadside or on a dunghill.

Until the middle of the nineteenth century the unmarried mother whose family and friends had forsaken her had little choice but to enter the workhouse with her child or the penitentiary without it. 'The joys and satisfactions of motherhood were not for those who had no right to be mothers, and the fate of the child was a secondary consideration.'[14]

But there were exceptional people who were prepared to take unmarried mothers into their own homes to help restore them, an act of kindness taking courage in the callous climate of the time. A Mrs. Tennant, of Clewer, near Windsor, gave the hospitality of her own home to women in such need. Her work was taken over in 1852 by the Clewer House of Mercy and expanded and developed by this Anglican sisterhood.

A revival of the Anglican religious orders for women gave fresh impetus to the establishment of penitentiaries and similar institutions. Nor were new enterprises in rescue work restricted to the Tractarian and Anglo-Catholic wing of the Church. In the eighteen-thirties a group of Evangelicals founded the Female Aid Mission and opened a home for women.

In 1848 an article criticizing the absence of co-ordination between the efforts of many charities appeared in the *London Quarterly Review*; it also raised the question of what role the Church should assume in a sphere previously left mainly to individual enterprise.

Three years later the Church Penitentiary Association was formed 'to promote the establishment and assist in the maintenance of Houses of Refuge and Penitentiaries for the reception and reformation of Fallen Women, Penitents, and, when desirable, to facilitate the emigration of such women'. The Association's ambition by 1858 was 'no Diocese without its Diocesan Penitentiary, its affiliated Penitentiaries and House of Refuge.'

At about the same time a Female Penitentiaries Special Fund gave direct practical help to women needing money, and a few years later this realistic body (which acquired the severe title, the Female Mission to the Fallen) pioneered the appointment of paid 'street missionaries' and provided accommodation for mothers with their babies.

Here was an awakening to the fact that rehabilitation in the community was an optimistic alternative to segregation from it. There was a new and enlightened move in the eighteen-sixties, supported by the Mission, to give short-term care to the nursing mothers, and provide long-term care, often a foster home, for the baby when the mother went out to work, usually into domestic service. But the mother was obliged to contribute to her utmost towards the child's upkeep. Nevertheless, this provision was criticized on the grounds that it was ridding mothers 'of a burden which they have brought upon themselves'.[15]

Progress against widespread public apathy and indifference to the plight of unmarried mothers and their offspring continued to be slow. Those who risked public displeasure by taking action often reaped only abuse for their humanitarian concern and always they were sensitive to the resentment which smouldered beneath public attacks upon their work.

Even the single-minded Dr. Barnardo (1845–1905) whose convictions sometimes brought an autocratic quality to his methods, was anxious not to alienate public support for his work. His Christian faith and personal courage were phenomenal, and he had a reverence for childhood which inspired him to become the outstanding befriender of destitute children, but along with a burning awareness of his mission went a cautious good sense about public relations. He knew he would be accused of encouraging immorality if he helped to relieve unmarried mothers of their responsibility and he was not convinced that to do so would be wise policy. Instead he believed the mother's love for her child to be the most powerful regenerating influence and that for this to be effective the mother should help support the child. He was loath to take illegitimate children into his Homes and in 1889 he started an auxiliary boarding-out scheme. Unmarried mothers agreed to enter domestic service and to place their babies in foster homes nearby so that they could spend their free time with their babies. Dr. Barnardo would help to pay the foster mother but if the natural mother relapsed into 'a vicious and immoral life' payments were to be stopped. There is no record of any case where this happened. The records may have been at fault, or, as appears more likely, Dr. Barnardo could not bring himself to withdraw help from a child because the mother had failed to keep her side of the agreement.

Social conditions in Barnardo's lifetime were appalling, especially in the cities. Children today are seldom abandoned physically, turned tatterdemalion out of their homes (their clothes and shoes at the pawnshop), hired or sold to tramps, or starved to death for the insurance money. Less than a hundred years ago such cruelties were commonplace. Evil women secured the custody, for a consideration, of unwanted children, took out an insurance policy on their lives, and then by a subtle process of neglect, ill-treatment and starvation, endeavoured to make sure that no undue time elapsed before the sum could be claimed. Destitute children taken into Barnardo's care, well-fed and clothed, would be inveigled away by some disreputable relative who would pawn the clothes and boots and thrust the child out into the streets again in the same wretched condition from which he had been rescued. Even those aware of these criminal abuses were reluctant to act. They were too timid, too uncertain to help, 'fearful lest they should unconsciously but none the less really become the ministers of sin, should make vice easy and relieve too readily the shoulders of those who have been alike foolish and sinful of the burden which should be alike their penalty for the past and their deterrent for the future'.[16]

Despite the immensity of the problem—there were 30,000 destitute children under sixteen in London alone[17]—Barnardo's have always kept to their audacious pledge of an ever-open door and no destitute child ever refused admission. When Dr. Barnardo opened his first home for boys in Stepney Causeway in 1870 he resolved to take in only as many boys as he felt able to provide for without incurring debts. Soon afterwards he refused a boy of eleven, who pleaded for admission, promising him the next vacancy. The child died from exhaustion and hunger and Barnardo vowed no child would ever again be turned away.

Utter destitution constituted the best claim for the admission of children to the 'Waifs and Strays', a dismal title but distressingly accurate in the situation when the society was founded in 1881 by Edward Rudolf, a young civil servant. Edward at nineteen, and his brother, Robert, at fifteen, became the superintendent and teacher of a Sunday school in Lambeth. For the next ten years they worked together among the starving and neglected children of London and determined to have a Church home, or orphanage, where these children would be brought up in the faith of the Church of England. The Archbishop of Canterbury, Dr. Tait, became the first president of the society devoted to waifs and strays and set a precedent which has continued. In 1946 the old 'Waifs and Strays' became the Church of England Children's Society and today helps about 5,000 children every year. Edward Rudolf's faith was matched by a practical vision which is also embodied in the present administration of the Church of England Children's Society. It aims to give its children a family life rather than an institutional one, adhering to Rudolf's principle of 'boarding out the children under guarantees for their proper maintenance and education in the principles of the Church of England'.

Boarding out in suitable homes was also a solution favoured by Dr. Barnardo. He was a pioneer in this as in almost every aspect of enlightened care of the destitute child. As early as 1886 he boarded out children in carefully selected cottage homes in the country with foster-parents of the right type—'kindly Christian folk who loved children and were prepared to take them to their hearts and not merely receive them for the maintenance payments'.[18]

The early visionaries certainly intended the children to have good substitute homes, but the security and love these children found was shattered by being taken away again too early.

The agreement with the foster-parents gave Dr. Barnardo the right to recall his children for vocational training at twelve, then the school-leaving age. The Thomas Coram Homes, then the Foundling Hospital, placed their babies in foster-homes but withdrew the children at an even earlier and more critical age. They were automatically recalled when they were five 'and any further contact between them and the foster-mothers depended on the persistence of the foster mothers'.[19]

It all seems cruelly unimaginative today but at that time there was no possibility of legal adoption. It is remarkable that in spite of the vast numbers of abandoned children, adoption did not seem to have occurred to anyone as a solution. Maybe the idea flowered and withered under the frosts of prejudice and piety which abhorred the acceptance of bastards.

*   *   *

In fact, the movement to legalize adoption was an oblique result of the 1914–18 war which robbed thousands of families of their sons and caused illegitimate births to reach a new peak. The war, with all its horror, stimulated acceptance of new ideas and broader sympathies. In 1919 a report, 'Rescue Work—an Enquiry and Criticism', published privately by the Committee of Social Investigation and Reform, was outspoken in its criticism of much so-called 'rescue work' which by then was widespread. 'With the outstanding exception of the Salvation Army and one or two other small attempts', said the report, 'it seems to be based on the conception that the individual has committed the worst of crimes and the best way to reclaim her is to so organize her life that it shall be spent in contemplation of the crime committed.'

This new search for a more liberal and compassionate attitude crystallized between the wars in the Adoption of Children's Act 1926 which legalized adoption but left room for abuses in the way it was carried out. Better safeguards for both children and adopters were achieved by later regulations which have been consolidated now in the 1959 Adoption Act.

Similar pressures upon established moral judgements and punitive attitudes followed the Second World War, and typical of the renewed criticism of the second post-war era were the views of 'Political and Economic Planning' upon church homes for unmarried mothers: 'The standards of the voluntary homes and the workers sponsored by these bodies are extremely variable and uncontrolled even by the central organizations with which they are associated. Some of the homes are excellent but many are extremely old-fashioned in building and personnel. Some work on free modern lines, others have locked doors, open all letters, remove pocket-money and notepaper... are virtually prisons and the more self-respecting girls would not want to enter them, even if they needed them badly.'[20] Homes were also criticized for being much too rigorous, imposing unreasonable discipline and too much heavy work. Diet, heating, and sanitary arrangements were considered of too low a standard for a woman in late pregnancy.

It was this kind of home which confirmed growing popular suspicions that moral welfare work had a strong punitive element and this could not be divorced from a religious approach. There was also the suggestion that moral welfare workers were exploiting the unmarried mother's need of care to indoctrinate her with unwanted religious beliefs and practices.

There is, of course, some historical justification for such pressure on the part of welfare workers, particularly those employed by religious organizations. Moral welfare work has its roots in rescue and reform, the ideals of spiritual and social rehabilitation. Naturally, many workers found it difficult to alter traditional outlooks to meet a new situation in which they were expected by most merely to give temporary shelter, adequate physical care and as speedy a discharge as possible.

The difficulties of welfare workers in moving with the times, however, did not make their overt or subtle pressures deriving from the past any the less distasteful to many they sought to help.

Nevertheless, however justified the criticism, the fact remains that all denominations of the Church were trying to look after unmarried mothers, and the expression of their help was slowly changing. The old disciplinarian 'refuges' were giving away at last to more modern mother and baby homes.

Motives for reform may have been mixed and confused, but it is indisputable that the inspiration of most early social care was religious and that the State was slow to assume any responsibility. It appears that the governments simply ignored the problems, for the mortality rate of illegitimate babies had long been presented as a cause for concern. In 1916 the Registrar-General drew attention to the increase in the ratio of illegitimate to legitimate infant mortality especially in the first week of life. He wrote in his report for that year: 'The facts suggest that infant welfare organizations might well devote special attention to the first few days in the life of the illegitimate child.' But it was not until 1943, when the illegitimacy figures had soared to new wartime heights, that the Ministry of Health placed responsibility for the care of unmarried mothers and their children on the local authorities.[21]

While acknowledging the achievements of the voluntary agencies, the Ministry pointed out that these bodies were not large enough for the task, nor were their services acceptable to all unmarried mothers. The Ministry asked that the welfare authorities should co-operate with the voluntary agencies and reinforce their work. They also suggested that every welfare authority should form its own schemes and appoint specialist workers to run them. By March 1945 schemes submitted by local authorities in England and Wales totalled 339; two-thirds of these local councils were working with voluntary bodies, fifty had appointed qualified workers, and others had placed a health visitor in charge of the work.[22]

c

This, of course, was a wartime effort to meet an alarming situation, an illegitimate birth-rate in 1945 of 9·3 per cent. After the war came a slide back to the old practices of relying upon district health visitors, reference to voluntary organizations of mothers with special difficulties or in need of residential care. By 1959, the Younghusband Committee on social workers in the Local Authority Health and Welfare Services reported a reluctance to accept direct responsibility for looking after unmarried mothers and their children: at that time only sixteen local authorities in England and Wales had special staff for this purpose.[23]

Today the children's departments of local authorities still have no specific responsibilities for the care of unmarried mothers and their babies over and above their duty to all children in need. In this field they continue to derive their authority from the Children's and Young Persons Act 1933 and the Children's Act 1948, although both have been amended from time to time.

The 1933 Act provides for the protection of children and young people under seventeen who, whether they have committed any offence or not, are in moral danger or beyond control. An Amendment in 1952 extended the Act's protection to children under seventeen who are neglected in a manner likely to cause them unnecessary suffering.

The 1948 Children's Act makes local authorities responsible for the care of children deprived of parents either temporarily or permanently. It also stipulates that every county council and county borough council must appoint a Children's Committee and a Children's Officer whose task it is to look after deprived children.

It is undeniable that some of the direct responsibility placed upon local authority services has been delegated, if it was ever assumed. Many local authorities continue to rely upon the voluntary organizations and workers instead of appointing their own specialist staff and providing their own facilities, although social work has become an exacting profession. Certainly it is less costly and altogether less onerous for an authority to subsidize a voluntary home even generously than to provide one of its own. But in England and Wales only 27 of the 171 homes for unmarried mothers and their babies are provided by local authorities. This can only amount to an unfortunate evasion of State responsibility. Also, the near monopoly of voluntary endeavour in the field may not only depress standards but help to perpetuate humiliating, unnecessary, and outworn concepts of charity. In 1966–7 voluntary agencies were caring for 4,877 children placed with them by local authorities[24] who consider meeting bills amounting to £1,855,684, an easy way of meeting their legal responsibilities.

This may sound a harsh judgement upon the loyal service many people render local government and it will be pointed out that the children placed with voluntary organizations represent only a small fraction of the total in local authority care. But nowhere are the impersonal attitudes behind so much of the administration that passes for grass roots democracy as productive of human misery as those that prevail in so-called 'welfare work' among distressed and problem families and deprived children. As so often happens, even official shafts of enlightenment fail to penetrate the gloom of entrenched practices. Maybe this is because established methods, however disastrous in some individual cases, always seem to be the most acceptable to the administrators.

A committee with Miss Myra Curtis as its chairman, published in 1946 the results of an inquiry into the care of children deprived of a normal home life. The Curtis Report, the first investigation of its kind in Britain, was welcomed widely for its progressive and discerning recommendations, but it still considered it sensible for babies to be cared for in residential nurseries. These the committee described as 'specially arranged to meet their needs and giving highly skilled specialized attention to their physical health'.

This showed an appalling disregard of weighty evidence which had been available for many years to show that babies and very young children thrive under individual attention and in an atmosphere of family affection.[25]

Nevertheless, the Curtis Report met with strong approval when it recommended adoption as serving best the older child's welfare and boarding-out as preferable to placing in a residential community, the last resort. The report also emphasized the extreme seriousness of taking a child away from even an indifferent home: 'Every effort should be made to keep the child in its home, or with its mother if it is illegitimate, provided that the home is or can be made reasonably satisfactory. . . . The aim of the authority must be to find something better—indeed much better—if it takes the responsibility of providing a substitute home.'[26]

Even those who tried to follow this sound advice were often frustrated by inflexible laws which curbed rather than encouraged initiative. The freedom to exercise such good sense and human kindness did not come until the Children and Young Persons Act of 1963. This invests local authorities with a clear duty to do all they can to keep families together. They must make available 'such advice, guidance, and assistance as may promote the welfare of children by diminishing the need to receive them into, or keep them in care, or for them to be brought before a juvenile court.'[27]

More importantly the Act provides for help to be given in kind or in cash, and so for example, has made it possible for a few enterprising local authorities to provide well-paid 'Substitute Mums' to look after families where the mother has deserted, or is ill, or dead. Practically, this means great financial economies compared with taking children into care, and in human terms the return in happiness when families are kept together is immeasurable. Cornwall has employed 'emergency mothers' since 1965, and so has Lewisham, the London borough, where the scheme was pioneered in 1962 only to be frustrated by the legislation existing at that time.

So far, however, the powers given to local authorities in 1963 have not succeeded in reversing the steadily rising number of children in their care and before the courts.

The most serious obstacle to pursuing new imaginative policies is probably the recruitment and training of staff of the high standard needed. Home Office figures reveal that only one-third of the child care officers required by local authorities could be recruited in 1964. Hours are long, responsibilities heavy, and salaries low. In 1962 the number of child-care officers with full professional qualifications was only 26 per cent of those employed, while 40 per cent were completely untrained.[28] Five years later fifty-one children's departments had no trained staff at all and another thirty-five departments had 20 per cent and less.[29]

But there is evidence that there is wasteful multiplication of effort in the whole field of social work—a problem family can be visited by a score of different welfare agencies—and it is plain that much can be done to involve us all in caring more. We need to care enough, every one of us, to ensure that no child today has to struggle to grow up, in emotional isolation, without the unconditional love of an ordinary family.

The Home Office was explicit that the 1963 legislation was framed 'to give scope for initiative and experiment by local authorities'. Certainly, the legislation now provides for fresh thinking which will cut through prejudices, complacency, and administrative delays. The need for new solutions and their introduction is the simple fact that the futures of thousands of children and their mothers depend upon renewed inspiration and action.

NOTES

1. Re *Ann Lloyd* (1841), 3 Manning & Granger, Maule J., at p. 548.
2. Wimperis, Virginia, *The Unmarried Mother and Her Child* (George Allen & Unwin, Ltd., 1960), 122.
3. Home Office.
4. Bastardy Laws Amendment Act.
5. Bastardy Act S.2.
6. Affiliation Orders Act.
7. Matrimonial Proceedings (Magistrates Courts) Act.
8. Re O. (an infant), 1 All E.R. 787. Lord Denning's judgment (1964).
9. In Re C. (an infant). Court of Appeal, 21 February 1966.
10 Court of Appeal, *Sydall* v. *Castings Ltd.*, 10 October 1966.
11. Court of Appeal, *Sydall* v. *Castings Ltd.*, 10 October 1966.
12. Massie, J., 'Observations relating to the Foundling Hospital Shewing the Ill Consequences of giving public support thereto', London (1758).
13. Hall, M. Penelope and Howes, Ismene V., *The Church in Social Work*, (Routledge & Kegan Paul, 1965).
14. Ferguson, S. M., and Fitzgerald, M., *Studies in the Social Service* (H.M.S.O., 1954), p. 80.
15. Annual Report, Female Mission to the Fallen, 1867.
16. Dyson, D. M., *No Two Alike* (George Allen & Unwin Ltd., 1962).
17. Williams, A. E., *Barnardo of Stepney* (George Allen & Unwin Ltd., 1943).
18. Williams, E. A., *Barnardo of Stepney* (George Allen & Unwin Ltd., 1943).
19. Dyson, D. M., *No Two Alike* (George Allen & Unwin Ltd., 1962).
20. Planning No. 255, 13 September 1946. In a survey in 1968, Jill

Nicholson writes in 'Mother and Baby Homes' (George Allen & Unwin): 'No wonder that the first impression of the Home confirmed the girls' worst fears that they were coming into a workhouse or a prison. . . .'

21. Ministry of Health Circular No. 2866, 16 November 1943.

22. Hall, M. Penelope and Howes, Ismene V., *The Church in Social Work* (Routledge & Kegan Paul, 1965).

23. Ibid.

24. Home Office, 'Children in Care in England and Wales', March 1967 (H.M.S.O.).

25. In 1938 the matter was publicly discussed in the League of Nations Report, League of Nations (1938). 'The Placing of Children in Families', (Geneva, 2 vols.).

26. 'The Curtis Report', p. 148, par. 447.

27. Home Office Circular No. 204/1963.

28. 'Manpower in the Child Care Service', Social Work, January 1964, p. 16.

29. *Child Care News*, February 1968, p. 17.

2

Unmarried Mothers

ALL that unmarried mothers have in common are illegitimate babies. Unmarried mothers are not all neurotic, sexually ignorant, good-time girls, or social misfits. They do not all scheme to ensnare a husband, long to fulfil their womanhood, or yearn after a love-object in a baby of their own. Their backgrounds, personalities, motives, and needs are as individual and varied as they are infinitely human.

To governments their needs and problems are lost in a few dull statistics. The Registrar-General provides the sole authoritative figures concerning illegitimate children and their parents but the information is sparse and inadequate. No attempt is made to provide a statistical basis for any purposive analysis at a national level.

There is desultory research into the causes of unmarried motherhood and the surveys which have been carried out are virtually useless. They are out of date and their irrelevance is heightened by the fact that social change is an accelerating process requiring more immediate analysis.

It is remarkable too that some of the studies which are most frequently quoted were carried out in other countries with different cultural influences and so cannot be totally relevant to life in Britain.

It is also readily apparent that most of the research relates to unrepresentative groups and, even if it were contemporarily applicable, would not provide a better understanding of the conduct and character of unmarried mothers who neither see psychiatrists nor turn to social agencies for help. In fact it is only a minority of unmarried mothers who seek help beyond family and friends or their doctors. Figures compiled in London in 1964 showed that only 39 per cent of unmarried mothers were seen by moral welfare organizations.[1]

The sum of all these researches is like a candle in a catacomb: outlines are discernible and shadows make bizarre pictures on the walls. The simple truth is that the research of the past thirty years variously confirms conflicting theories. Unmarried mothers are found to be constant and to have a deep and often long-lasting love affair with one man, and also to be promiscuous. They are neurotic in one sample, and remarkably normal in another. One sociologist discovers that they come mostly from the artisan classes, and a second that the professional classes are there but camouflaged. Young girls are the most psychologically scarred by the experience, and at the same time resilient enough to be unharmed.

A study of the unmarried mothers in a Midland town in 1950 (disguised as 'Midborough' although the need for anonymity is obscure) showed that most of the fathers of illegitimate babies were either the fiancé or a steady friend of the mother. Fewer than 20 per cent had known the man less than a year. The father was termed a casual acquaintance by only a score of mothers out of some 250. But it is hardly to be expected that many would admit to sexual intercourse with a mere acquaintance. When the baby was conceived about half the single mothers were living with the father, and of those who were married, widowed, or divorced nearly three-quarters were living together. For more than a quarter of these 'Midborough' mothers the baby was a second or later child born in an unofficial family by the same father. Five years later many of the mothers had more illegitimate children but mostly the father was the same man as before. Only 7 per cent had had illegitimate children by more than one man.

In Birmingham, in 1955, more than half of the unmarried mothers known to the city's Maternity and Child Welfare Department were living with the father and child as an ordinary family. Other inquiries around the same date showed that 40 per cent of the illegitimate children in a Newcastle-on-Tyne survey and 30 per cent of those studied in Kilmarnock were living with both unmarried parents.

So the picture emerges of the unmarried mother remarkably faithful to one man, but she is painted in a different light by a Swiss doctor, Professor Hans Binder, whose work was published in Switzerland in 1941.[2] His inquiries among 350 unmarried women revealed more than half to be promiscuous in varying degrees. He found that 35 per cent, the largest single group, had frequent sex relations in one or more affairs and 17 per cent were entirely promiscuous. The girl's sexual relations with the baby's father often began soon after her acquaintance with him. Nearly half admitted that intercourse had occurred at their first or one of their first meetings. Most of the women had had only one illegitimate child, 11 per cent two, and 3 per cent more than two.

Professor Binder found that 3 per cent of the women in his study were quite ignorant sexually; 22 per cent had sexual relations with the child's father only; and 16 per cent had only isolated sex experience springing from chance meetings at dances and parties, out of bravado, curiosity, a desire to please, and often when drunk. But in his view 90 per cent of these unmarried mothers had an exaggerated desire to be loved.

An earlier survey of unmarried mothers in Germany by Weinzierl in 1925 claimed that 80 per cent of the unmarried mothers had had no other lover, but Professor Binder, with a realistic worldliness, was inclined to ascribe this to the fact that Weinzierl had only the mother's word for it.

Professor Binder claimed that his group of unmarried mothers was unselected and representative, an assertion which must be challenged. He chose at random 350 cases from a register of 3,000 illegitimate births since 1912 on the files of the Official Guardianship Bureau of Basle. Obviously, only effective contacts could be included and there is the possibility that many who did not answer his letter or refused to be interviewed were of higher mental and social level than those who did co-operate.

An American researcher in the field, Dr. Leontine Young, cannot claim to have investigated a cross-section of unmarried motherhood. She took a random sample of a hundred mothers aged eighteen to forty from an unmarried mothers' agency, excluding those who came from a background where illegitimacy was 'socially acceptable' and any mothers under the age of eighteen.[3] She found all of them had grown up to have fundamental problems in their relationships with other people. Few were promiscuous and only a quarter of the group had had more than a fleeting relationship with the child's father. Hardly any of them had genuinely cared for or been happy with their lover. In all these women there appeared a strong unconscious desire to become pregnant.

Dr. Young was emphatic that most unmarried mothers were neurotic, the child being a symptom of the neurosis. She concluded that they were frequently bedevilled by an urge for self-punishment, or a need to use the baby as a weapon of retribution against unsympathetic parents. Others craved for someone to love, something which they had never known.

In a later book[4] Dr. Young was categoric in her determinist philosophy. Of the unmarried mother she wrote: 'To say that her behaviour is the result of immorality or from free choice is to ignore all the evidence. The logical and seemingly inevitable result of her psychological development is an out-of-wedlock child, and like a sleep-walker she acts out what she must do without awareness or understanding of what it means or of the fact that she plans and initiates the action.'

Dr. Young also found that the older woman who became an unmarried mother tended to be more neurotic than the young girl because our society condemned her with more violence than the girl.

On the other hand, Professor Binder found that unmarried motherhood had the most permanent ill-effects on young girls. His study aimed to discover the extent of the psychological damage wrought by the experience of unmarried motherhood. By the time he interviewed the woman in his study—more than half had had their baby ten years earlier—half of them had still not regained their 'inner equilibrium' and had turned into more or less abnormal people as a result of their chronic inner conflicts and social and economic difficulties. A third of the women were becoming fairly seriously warped psychologically, and in 7 per cent the damage was severe. He concluded that favourable psychic developments as a result of unmarried maternity were rare and only happened in women who were already reasonably stable people.

Yet more conflicting evidence is offered about the vulnerability of young girls by a study at St. Mary's Hospital, Manchester, of sixty-two unmarried girls under eighteen years old, carried out between January 1953 and March 1955. With few exceptions the girls showed no psychiatric abnormalities and went through their pregnancy uneventfully.

Statistics are lamentably uninstructive but a number of research projects have indicated that more illegitimate children are born to the artisan classes. Less than 10 per cent of Midborough's mothers are believed to have had a secondary education and most of the women were housewives and factory workers. A study of illegitimate births in Aberdeen, 1949–52, made by Barbara Thompson,[5] showed that the incidence of illegitimacy rose from 2 per cent in the professional and technical group to 19 per cent among the catering and cleaning workers. Nevertheless, it is possible that many more professional women have illegitimate babies than these figures suggest.

Women of the middle and upper classes are more mobile, have more money, more education, more experience of the world and perhaps more widely distributed friends and relatives. For many of them abortion is not an economic or a social impossibility. It should also be remembered when considering the results of researches in various places that it is not unusual for a mother to have an illegitimate baby somewhere where she is unknown. She may also insist upon the birth being registered where the baby is born, and this could be one reason why some London areas and many coastal resorts have illegitimate birth-rates high above the average.

Through this complex of fragmentary evidence and interpretation runs one strongly disturbing common thread. There is appalling unanimity to support the observation that the problem of unmarried parenthood is self-generating: an unhappy childhood tends to produce a new generation of irresponsible if not unmarried parents. Children denied a warm and secure family life find it difficult to mature into strong and loving parents themselves.

A large number of unmarried mothers started with a poor inheritance. They came from broken homes and often had histories of illegitimacy or institutional life. They knew quarrelling parents and lacked affection and security. These early experiences handicapped their chances to make genuine friendships and courtships in adult life. Professor Binder found that nearly 40 per cent of the unmarried mothers in his study had lost one or both parents before they became pregnant, and 28 per cent before they were fifteen. When they became pregnant 42 per cent had no connection with their homes at all; another 21 per cent had long left home although still in touch with their families, and the rest were living with their parents or foster-parents. But they were living a relatively unprotected life and few had come from a home that was happy or normal.

In Dr. Young's sample of a hundred unmarried mothers in New York all except six came from broken homes or had parents who were dominating or rejecting, or both.

Barbara Thompson's study also establishes that a preponderance of unmarried mothers came from broken homes. As many as 40 per cent in her study grew up in homes in which one or other parent was missing, or did not grow up in their parental home at all. Her study also noted that those without a father figure were twice as many among unmarried mothers and that the fathers of illegitimate children often came from broken homes themselves.

Apart from illustrating how this legacy of unhappiness punishes innocent generations yet unborn in a vicious circle of destructiveness, the researches are seen to be obsolete and contradictory and without much reference to the nineteen-sixties in Britain. Unlike wine, research does not improve with keeping. Traditionalists will argue that human nature does not change and so the studies are timeless and placeless in their significance. But it is clear that human behaviour is affected by cultural changes and the pressures exerted by our society have radically altered since the Second World War. Yet outdated research is still revered by the experts, and there is a reluctance to discard theories worn thin by time and change. There is also the danger that experts are more prone to confer with their colleagues than with their clients.

At a conference on the unmarried mother and her child in 1966,[6] the time of several hundred doctors and social workers, many of whom had travelled long distances to reach London, was wasted by one eminent speaker who merely recapitulated the findings of a study of sixty-two adolescent girls whose illegitimate babies were born in Manchester between January 1953 and March 1955. Another speaker recounted in considerable detail a follow-up study of illegitimate children born in the former London County Council area between April 1953 and May 1954.

At the same conference Dr. Donald Gough, psycho-analyst and consultant psychiatrist to mother and baby homes, placed the unmarried mother in a 'special group' because she had failed to make use of the 'widespread possibilities of contraceptives and abortion'. Surely a remarkable view because it is far from easy for an unmarried woman to equip herself with effective contraception. At that time it was only becoming openly possible at all through the services of the Brook Advisory Centre operating in London and one or two provincial cities with long waiting-lists. Now the Family Planning Association may also advise the unmarried, and local authorities were empowered in June 1967 to make contraceptives available to all. It will be interesting to see how these new opportunities are exploited. At present a single girl still needs both resolution and initiative to obtain safe contraceptives and should she fail, money and influence for a medical abortion.[7] Nor is it probable, despite their distress, that many girls of sensibility with ordinary maternal feelings wish to end the life of their unborn child. Many will feel ambivalent in their attitude to the baby: only a minority revulsion and anguish enough to destroy it.

All unmarried mothers feel guilt about illegitimate children and this often expresses itself in obsessive anxiety that the baby will be born deformed. After the child is born the mothers nearly always reverse, at least temporarily, any previous decision to part with their babies. If a mother parts from her baby there is a great need in the weeks following for her to mourn her lost child and much depends upon her ability to do this successfully. These mothers are most in need of help immediately after the baby's coming, but frequently social workers do not feel free to keep in close touch with them once they have gone into hospital.

Too often charity as practised in our society carries the over-tones of revenge, instead of embracing forgiveness and acceptance, both essential to emancipate and restore the individual from guilt and depression. Many of the mother and baby homes founded by the Church were run in ways which expressed punitive charity, and only twenty years ago were criticized for resembling prisons, imposing unreasonable discipline and too heavy work.[8] There have been many improvements, but an acute problem is recruiting suitable and adequate staff. Most of the domestic work is still done by the residents and fees are often kept low at the expense of heavily pregnant girls cleaning the stairs.

A memorandum on residential homes in 1964[9] said: 'There is sometimes residual punitiveness and a demand that girls should feel gratitude, and staff and committee members have been known to express the view that conditions in the homes are too comfort-able. . . . There is sometimes lack of knowledge about administer-ing permissive discipline and occasionally punishments which seem unsuitable for adults or adolescents are imposed.' Visits from parents are usually welcomed, but the attitude of superinten-dents to visits from the baby's father or other boy friends is usually discouraging.

Whatever the shortcomings of modern mother and baby homes, and they are not remarkable for their capacity to meet the individual needs of the mother, it is a fact that many girls draw strength and comfort from the companionship of others facing the same stark situation. They would probably feel even more sup-ported if the baby could be born in the 'Home' which after some weeks provides the reassurance of the familiar. They may also have found friends among staff and inmates with whom there is no call for pretence or embarrassment. But only about a fifth of the 'Homes' are also Maternity Hospitals.

Many unmarried mothers stay with relatives or friends through-out their pregnancies. Theoretically, such support should be valuable to the girl but it may well be that a relation or friend can be too censorious or too enveloping at this highly emotional time.

Both are harmful attitudes and do nothing to help the girl to mature.

Mothers at the extremes of child-bearing age are often unsuitable for care in Mother and Baby Homes. Very young mothers may interpret being sent away to a 'Home' as rejection and punishment, particularly if it is the first time they have been away from home. Older women consider themselves too old for the rules of any institution and may be too self-conscious to share such a private experience with many younger girls, who often find emotional relief by forming cliques and exchanging confidences among themselves.

With child mothers, who are in sore need of mothering themselves, and with women of mature years, the ideal arrangement appears to be carefully selected 'foster-homes' where the mother can stay before her confinement and with the baby afterwards for as long as necessary, and where the mother may welcome the baby's father, her family and friends. A number of local authorities and social agencies approve 'fostering' of this kind. Unfortunately such foster-homes are extremely hard to find. There is a deep-seated reluctance to act as foster-parents/landladies because of the worries attached to the situation and its influence on younger children. It stirs up, too, all the latent and phantom fears and jealousies that sexual behaviour in the young brings out in most of us.

There is much controversy about whether or not a mother who has decided upon adoption for her child should see her baby. Some believe it is not possible for her to make and accept a final decision about the baby's future unless she has known him as a real person. There is evidence that some mothers who have never seen their babies later find themselves unable to sign their consent to adoption, or, grieving for the baby they never cradled, they get themselves a replacement baby.

On the other hand, mothers who are required to look after their babies for some time—many mother and baby homes enforce a three months' stay of six weeks before and after the confinement—find this long personal involvement emotionally capsizing. They may even change their minds about an adoption which made good sense, although they have small hope of themselves being able to care for their babies successfully.

Of course, the mother's emotional and social needs vary and no single solution is likely to be universally or totally acceptable. But there is a tendency to stereotype unmarried mothers instead of valuing them as individuals of varying capacities to mature and with different depths of maternal feelings.

Suffering is inherent in the situation and those trying to help often try to protect themselves from painful involvement by pretending that an unmarried mother's feelings have less depth and quality. When the mother is young, social workers sometimes identify with her parents and almost disallow her to come into the situation in an attempt to protect her. Parents too sometimes make the mistake of trying to shield their daughter by shouldering the responsibility almost totally and presenting her with a cut-and-dried plan. Over-protection of this kind brings long-term difficulties for the girl, who feels the decisions must be of her own making, and one justified criticism of third-party arrangements is that the mother is committed to a plan without feeling an important part of it.

More care and thought could also be brought to the manner of the mother's parting with her infant. It is unnecessarily harrowing for a girl to wait in the sitting-room of a 'Home' while strangers come to see if they want her cherished baby, or to make a lonely journey to an office to surrender her baby dressed in his best gown.

There are attractive arguments to be made that the situation becomes warmer and more human if the natural mother meets the adoptive parents. The mother is helped to make a firm decision and haunting fears of faceless people taking her child are quelled. The adopters would also be helped if later they wished to give their child some sort of personal portrait of his own mother and why she was unable to bring him up herself. Understanding the facts can prevent the adopted child from inventing fantasies which are often more frightening than unhappy reality; but on the whole these arguments indulge the adult emotions involved and are of doubtful relevance to the real need of the child, a home.

The permanence and love that an adoptive home should give is a happy solution for an illegitimate child but it should not be regarded as a panacea. Many more mothers would keep their illegitimate children if there were more and better services to help them do so, and if they were convinced that the community would not be hostile towards them both. Only about a quarter of their illegitimate babies are adopted but it is a comfortable myth that the rest live happily and securely with their own mothers.

Many unmarried mothers filled with valiant intentions fail to surmount the financial and social hurdles they meet and ask for adoption to be arranged when the baby is many months old. By this time the parting is even more grievous for both, and the adopters are likely to be presented with a difficult baby who has too long been the emotional centre of vacillation and heartbreak.

Other unmarried mothers can never bring themselves to let their children go. Unable to establish a satisfactory home for the child and themselves, and emotionally incapable of allowing others completely to take their place, they deny the child mother and home and leave him deprived of both in an institution. Here his sense of deprivation is heightened by the occasional visits of his natural mother as a special stranger who brings sweets and toys. Worse still, nobody comes and utter desolation may enclose him.

Parents are indeed vital to children and if they do not have any substitutes they often invent them as a defence mechanism and to win status within the institution. Obviously, no one, however kind, can be a substitute for parents who never appear, and so these children are often pathetically loyal to their shadowy mothers and sometimes resent a foster-mother because they suspect her of abduction or at least of preventing them from returning to their real mothers.

Many of the children in institutional care are boarded out, and, of course, often settle down happily with foster-parents whom they grow to love. They are secure in all but one important respect: there is nothing to prevent a strange woman, legally entitled to call herself 'Mother' coming at any time to carry the child away. This happens infrequently if the casework has been good but too often children are returned time and again from

D

foster-homes because of soiling the bed, or rudeness to the neighbours, or pilfering from the shops, and even from the foster-
parents themselves. Most commonly they are sent back because
they cannot give quickly enough to their foster-parents the reward
they expect: affection and gratitude. It is a vicious spiral of unhappiness. The deprivation of these children has made them difficult
and the effect produces further damage as they are once again
expelled from the warmth and stimulation of an ordinary home
and returned to an institution.

A mother who privately arranges a foster-home for her child
must inform the local authority unless the home is only temporary.
If a woman who is not a relative looks after a child for reward for
longer than a month then, legally, the home becomes a foster-
home under the supervision of the Local Authority. The shadow of
authority is evaded, however, if a child is kept for a month, sent
away for a few days, and then returns. Or if a fresh foster-mother
is found every month.

Often mothers make arrangements for a daily child-minder.
But too often all these provisions are so haphazard that the
bewildered child is passed from one woman to another and finds
little or no security in life.

A daily 'minder', who takes only one or two children does not
have to be registered or approved. Not surprisingly perhaps, there
are officially approved child-minders; but in fact these are so rare
that in 1966 only three of them could be found among Bristol's
population of nearly half a million. The explanation is that the
rules and regulations governing registration are as unrealistic as
they are rigorous, particularly in the poorer neighbourhoods
where the need for 'minders' is greatest. A registered child-minder
must provide each child with twenty-five square feet of play area
and as a fire precaution the children must all take their midday
rest downstairs.

Day nurseries cannot meet the heavy demand for places and
will rarely accept children on a part-time basis, although many
mothers on part-time work would like to use them this way and
so see more of their children.

The few local authority day nurseries that do exist are heavily subsidized. So we have the ludicrous position that we are actually paying to separate a mother from her baby during the time he needs her most when we could keep them together at no extra cost. More serious and more costly is the parallel situation of public care in institutions. To keep a baby in a residential nursery costs £12 a week and yet the baby mourns his mother and suffers grievously from his abandonment.

The system of indirect subsidies by way of nurseries and institutions is possibly preferred by many people because public opinion is too uncharitable to give without extracting a penalty. On the other hand social security allowances, comparatively unadvertised, recognize the fact that parting a mother from her baby is too heavy a penalty for both to pay. An outright gift to an unmarried mother may be looked upon as condoning bad conduct and would certainly rankle some other mothers respectably married or widowed but struggling to make ends meet. In all the circumstances, and not least because of the lack of child-minding and nursery services, the immediate problems of finding accommodation and a job can be insoluble to a mother who wants to keep her illegitimate baby.

Domestic service, with the child in tow, does promise some sort of solution; but many unmarried mothers are quite unsuited for it, and it takes experience and capability to combine the role of a mother with the duties of a paid servant. Sometimes, too, the mother is exploited as cheap labour on account of the employer's 'tolerance' of the baby.

Any young couple with children find it difficult to get lodgings or flats. Landladies are even more chary of a girl on her own with a baby, and if she finds rooms and a job and a place for her baby in a day-nursery, she can still face serious difficulties. She may fall ill, or the child may and need her full-time care.

It is sometimes suggested that two or three unmarried mothers should join forces to run a flat, but they are still unattractive tenants to most business landlords.

It is tempting, of course, to believe that all would be well if only the mother could take the baby to her parents' home and yet there both the mother and the child can become the centre of tensions.

Again, even if the arrangement works well, all too often the child is so completely taken over by his grandmother that he comes to regard her as his 'mother', and his mother as a sister, and so is profoundly shocked when later he discovers the true relationships. Fortunately, there are signs that these problems are at last beginning to be better appreciated. Practical solutions, however, are still painfully slow to emerge.

The National Council for the Unmarried Mother and Her Child exists to help mothers who do not want to give up a beloved baby merely because of practical considerations of means and housing. The Council also works towards the greater acceptance of unmarried mothers and their children within society. There are too few pioneering services, such as the Coram Foundation for Children which fosters babies for mothers who cannot have their children with them at once, or who need time to determine their plans. Some local authorities are now letting council houses and flats to unmarried mothers. Also there are housing schemes which offer independent flatlets and communal nurseries for working mothers, but about forty of these projects are held up for planning permission or lack of money. Uncharitably, many people condemn unmarried mothers whatever they do. If they keep the baby they are trollops; if they give the baby for adoption they are hard-hearted and 'unnatural'.

It is painfully certain that while 'charity' to the children is respectable and well-subscribed, 'charity' to their mothers is unpopular and neglected. Moreover, it is often overlooked that it takes two to create this poignant dilemma of babies without parents who can cherish them. Their fathers have no obvious need for medical or social care but large numbers may need sex education and psychological help. Research suggests that many unmarried fathers had rootless and loveless childhoods, but common sense also suggests that more young men are mesmerized by the sexual titillation of popular culture.

Sexual intercourse is experienced by one boy in three before he reaches eighteen, and far more alarming is the discovery that boys are unwilling to use contraception because this is regarded as 'unmanly', 'chicken', or spoiling pleasure.

Happily, many social workers are finding that the presumed father is not always a villain and often is capable of a remarkably caring attitude. Fathers of illegitimate children in this country have increasing legal rights. There are now powerful arguments to be made for increasing their responsibilities too. What can they do to redeem a situation which engulfs so many in deep unhappiness?

NOTES

1. London Administrative County Vital Statistics, 1964. Report of the County Medical Officer of Health and Principal School Medical Officer for 1964.

2. Hans Binder, *Uneheliche Mutterschaft*, 1941.

3. Young, Leontine, 'Personality Patterns in unmarried mothers', *Family Journal of Casework*. (Family Service Association of America, New York, 1945.)

4. Young, Leontine, *Out of Wedlock* (McGraw-Hill Publishing Co., 1954).

5. Thompson, Barbara, 'Social Study of Illegitimate Maternities'. (*British Journal of Social and Preventive Medicine*, April 1956.)

6. A day conference on the 'Unmarried Mother and Her Child' in Relation to Adoption, organized by the Medical Group of the Standing Conference of Societies Registered for Adoption, 26 October 1966.

7. On 27 April 1968, the Abortion Act became law. The 'social' clause of the Act permits abortion where there is 'risk of injury to the physical or mental health of the pregnant woman or any existing children'. But doctors disagree, there appears likely to be long waiting lists, and in practical terms it may well be as difficult as it was before to get a National Health service abortion.

8. Political and Economic Planning, No. 255. 13 September 1966.

9. 'Staffing in Residential Homes and Institutions, February 1964', National Council for the Unmarried Mother and Her child.

3

Unmarried Fathers

UNMARRIED fathers, like single mothers, cannot be put easily into one category, but a high proportion of them are unstable, immature characters whose own family life has been dispiriting. Probably they are more promiscuous than unmarried mothers. Michael Schofield's survey of the sexual behaviour of youth[1] says one boy in three has experienced sexual intercourse before eighteen, compared with fewer than one girl in five. Many of these boys despise the use of contraceptives—they 'don't like them', 'don't care'—and 40 per cent of them give no serious thought to the prospect of a baby from their love-making. Asked what they would do if their girl-friend was going to have a baby, these boys replied: 'Don't know' or 'it couldn't happen.' Pregnancy is a much more real contingency to a girl than a boy and only a few girls had not faced the question. If the girl has a baby a boy will often say: 'I deeply regret that this baby is coming into the world but I have no regrets that we had sexual intercourse.'

It seems clear that at last a distinction must be forced between immorality and promiscuous sexual behaviour, and it no longer goes unchallenged that the two are synonymous. The boy has a troubled conscience that he has caused an unwanted baby to be born: he is unrepentant that he has enjoyed sex. This is a common attitude and must receive serious attention from all those concerned with sex education.

Schofield's research is also revealing in this matter. He found that 86 per cent of schoolgirls were receiving sex education compared with 47 per cent of the boys.[2] The boys are even worse off at home. Parents try to help 71 per cent of daughters but only 33 per cent of sons.

The assumption that boys are sexually ineducable or incapable of acting responsibly in their sex life seems widespread. It is supported by the trite convention that young men should sow their wild oats and the double standards of morality for men and women which still persist.

Fathers of illegitimate children tend to be several years older than unmarried mothers, about a third of whom are twenty to twenty-four years old. Schoolboy fathers are far rarer than schoolgirl mothers. Of fifty unmarried teenage fathers interviewed by Captain Fred Smith of the Church Army in the last two years, most were about nineteen (9 were fifteen or sixteen; 6, seventeen; and 13 were eighteen). Fifty per cent of these boys had sex with girls of sixteen or under.

The average age of alleged fathers taken from the files of the Salvation Army over five months in 1967 was twenty-eight years old. Those interviewed by an adoption agency in 1916 averaged twenty-five years old. In another survey[3] of 278 men the largest group of fathers (22 per cent) were thirty to thirty-four years; 21 per cent twenty-five to twenty-nine years; 20 per cent twenty to twenty-four years; and 17 per cent between forty and forty-nine. Three-quarters of the women under thirty in this investigation had their babies by men within five years of their own age. None of the teenagers bore a child to a man over thirty.

English law is extraordinarily lenient towards the fathers of bastards. In most countries the illegitimate child has more than a legal right to money from his natural father; he has definite social and psychological claims too. Men who father bastards can 'recognize' them legally, without legitimizing the birth through adoption or subsequent marriage. An entry by the father in the public register of Births and Deaths is a formal declaration which creates a valid relationship between him and his illegitimate child.

Bastards whose fathers do not voluntarily 'recognize' them are legally entitled on the Continent to claim against their father's estates, and this is a right which devolves in turn upon their children. Often, bastards' rights are protected by a 'guardian' appointed by a court or local authority as soon as the child is born, and it is contended that without such guardians the children would be the losers. This is real 'filiation'. English law gives no rights to bastards. They have no legal claim even to the barest maintenance from their fathers. The unmarried father is customarily regarded as merely an uncertain source of money for the mother or public authority maintaining the child. Usually he is not pursued with much determination by either.

In this country perhaps 10 per cent of unmarried mothers obtain affiliation orders. Too often, they are reluctant and afraid to become involved in a court case; or so emotionally confused that they lack the energy and realism required to start legal proceedings. Many an unmarried mother hopes to marry the father of her child, or knowing he is married already still wants to protect him. Other women react violently against the father. They will not ask for money from a man who refuses them love and seems determined to deny his share in their child.

These emotions are understandable, even if they serve pride more often than the child's best interests. For a short time after having her baby, the unmarried mother can easily underestimate the difficulties of supporting him alone. Unfortunately, these first reactions can jeopardize the child's whole future. Normally, the unmarried mother must apply for an affiliation order before the child is a year old.[4] Indeed, if she wants maintenance back-dated to his birthday she must apply before the child is eight weeks old.

English law assumes a man to be the father of a bastard if he had sexual intercourse with the woman during the period of conception, unless he can produce evidence that another man had taken her within that time. The unmarried mother must instigate the proceedings and produce some corroborative evidence. This means that the man's best defence, unless he can prove inaccessibility, is to blacken the woman's character. A girl may go through the ordeal of a court hearing at risk that in order to destroy her case friends of the father may give false evidence of having slept with her. If this can be proved, neither the presumed father nor any other man is held responsible.

The expression 'affiliation order' appeared in English law for the first time in 1914 and it meant 'an order made under the Bastardy Laws Amendment Act, 1872 . . . adjudging a man to be the putative father of a bastard child and ordering him to pay a sum of money . . .'[5] In fact, the use of the term 'affiliation' is misleading. It disguises the extraordinary injustice that in English law there never has been any possibility of according a bastard a legal father. The natural father's legal responsibilities, slight as they are, relate only to the woman he has 'wronged'. He has no duties towards the child and it is remarkable that there is no provision in the law instructing an unmarried mother to spend the amount of an affiliation order directly for the child's benefit. Nevertheless, it is possible for others caring for a child whose mother has died or abandoned him, to receive money under an affiliation order. This applies to individuals, agencies, and councils.

There are limitations and objections to the European practice. Certainly the extent of the father's obligations and duties varies widely. Nevertheless, it is clear that in many other countries men do not have the same opportunity to behave irresponsibly towards their bastard children, to escape without penalty.

Continental ideas influenced recommendations by the Church of England in 1966 when a study group[6] advocated two major legal reforms in the interests of the illegitimate child. Fathers of bastards, it was suggested, should voluntarily be able to assume legal paternal responsibility for their children. If they do not, and the interests of the child seem in jeopardy, then the father should be brought into court. The study group's report argues that a child can belong in an ordinary legal sense to both a father and a mother. Even if born out of wedlock and not later legitimized by his parents' marriage or by adoption, he may still have legal parents as does a child of separated or divorced parents. After all, thousands of children live with natural parents who cohabit and are unconcerned that the law recognizes no kinship between the children and their fathers.

The right to take legal action for filiation should be conceded to bastards in Britain in the same way as is general on the Continent. Only the historical concept that bastards are the children of no one stands in the way.

If this reform is adopted, and there is every reason for doing so, then the illegitimate child will also need a legal guardian. Rights are one thing, achieving them another. Obviously, the best person to act for a baby disowned by his natural father will normally be the mother, but a reformed law should provide machinery which safeguards as many of the child's interests as possible. This means going beyond some simple provision of a legal guardian should the child's mother die or forsake him. A bastard's legal friend should be able to institute a search for the father and to start affiliation proceedings on behalf of a child who has not been 'recognized', nor had proceedings instituted by his mother soon after his birth. Such powers would remove from unmarried mothers an important freedom, the opportunity to do nothing to give the child any contact with his natural father. Often this seems justifiable to the mother because of her feelings of injured pride and anger, or lingering regard for the father. On the other hand, the present state of the law is over-indulgent towards the natural parents at the expense, if not total sacrifice, of the children's fortunes. It is easy to forget that the helpless and unfortunate baby should be the central object of concern.

Of course many unmarried fathers support bastards without affiliation orders. Possibly a third of them live in normal families with both their natural parents. Also, many men send the mother regular contributions towards the maintenance and if their arrangement is set out in a legal document so much the better.

No one knows how many of these private agreements are made. They have the advantage that if the father can afford it a much more generous sum may be secured for the child. The maximum a magistrate can impose under an affiliation order is fifty shillings a week even if the father is a 'Pop' singer earning a thousand pounds a week. The disadvantage of private agreements is the cost of bringing a case into county court should the father default. Few unmarried mothers can afford litigation, and if the man fails to pay, the agreement may have no value except as evidence of acknowledged paternity.

Continental courts are not restricted to a maximum award for affiliation, and in April 1968 a Government Committee recommended that statutory financial limits should be abolished in Britain. A number of countries also provide for maintenance payments to be continued once the child is grown-up should he prove unable to earn his living through physical or mental infirmity.

In Switzerland, where both parents are held to be equally liable, the father's contribution will depend on their joint resources. This is a logical expression of the aim of the courts to ensure that the child gets an upbringing in accord with the status of the parents. In Germany the father is primarily liable and the amount he has to pay depends on the social position of the mother. Often the European position is that the child should be brought up as befits the standing of both parents, or of the wealthier.

Social workers in this country suggest it would be difficult to get average wage-earners, the most frequent contributors under affiliation orders, to pay more than present awards. The argument is that orders for higher payments would lead to larger arrears when the prevention of this is the best way of safeguarding the financial future of the unmarried mother and her child. This seems a negative and pessimistic attitude. In fact, the records of two large city courts show that nearly all the orders fully honoured over many years were those for the higher sums.[7] The sum fixed is usually much less than the fifty shillings a week maximum, yet even so, many men fall into arrears with impunity. Only about 8 per cent of mothers are awarded the present maximum. The average award in 1966 was thirty-three shillings, and a third of the mothers who apply still get less than twenty-five shillings. In 1966 a third of affiliation orders were at least £20 in arrears, and a quarter of them fell into arrears within six months of being made.

The unmarried mother must request the Court to summons the father in arrears, and at the hearing both of them are expected to be present. In most cases the man is ordered to pay the outstanding sum, or a weekly amount off the arrears, and the case is adjourned for two or three months. Should he still fail in the payments there may be a further adjournment and then, finally, he may be sent to prison for not more than six weeks.

Imprisonment used to be regarded as payment of the debt although neither the child nor his mother benefited. On the contrary, the man on release was often more bitterly resolved not to pay. The stupidity of this was at last realized in 1958 when a new

Maintenance Orders Act provided that imprisonment for arrears did not wipe out the debt. Incredibly, the Act also embodied the principle that a man might not be imprisoned again for the out-standing debts, only for arrears incurred after release.

The 1958 Act also gave the courts new powers to recover arrears. If a man becomes a month behind with his payments, the court, on the woman's written request, may make 'an attachment of earnings order' to stop some of his wages at source.[8] And yet evasion is still easy. A man has only to change his job and district, to become unemployed or self-employed, or 'disappear'. If a bastard's father is missing the police can take little action and if he has gone abroad they must await his return.

With such inviting loopholes open to the father, the unmarried mother's affiliation order is often little better than a rubber cheque, although the child's needs are as constant as his father's help may be erratic.

Scandinavian countries in particular show more realistic under-standing of the money problems facing single mothers. As long ago as 1888 a scheme of State advances was working in Denmark where it became the forerunner of family allowances. At first the State's advances were solely to help illegitimate children but now they are paid for children whose parents have been divorced or separated. Such advances are not recoverable from the mother. They are treated as a debt the father owes to the public purse.

More than a third of all bastards receive these payments and about half of the money is successfully recovered. Powers to order how the money is spent and to ensure that these instructions are obeyed is vested in the Danish Child Welfare Committee.

No scheme for a welfare agency to underwrite payments promised under affiliation orders has yet been agreed in this country. The difficulties said to be in the way of this advance are both puny and pitiful.[9] It is claimed any legal proceedings taken by the welfare agency would require the consent of a committee and so there might often be delays. Also, that the father's sense of personal responsibility might be diminished in some way. At worst, he would make no effort to pay if he knew his bastard and the mother would automatically receive money.

Of the first objection all that need be said is that administrative delays which affect the economic security of mothers and young children should not be tolerated, let alone regarded as inevitable. The more important point is the question of the unmarried father's attitude towards his responsibility for maintenance. If the man has already stopped paying, it cannot be claimed that he has shown much concern anyway. Indeed, it could be argued that a system of State advances might give him a shock because a debt to the State can be more frightening than owing money to an individual. The State can bring massive pressure to bear, as the tenacity of the Inland Revenue department in this country constantly demonstrates. Nor need sanctions against the defaulting unmarried father be limited merely to a threat of imprisonment if he can be found for trial and sentence. Perhaps some new penalties would help: he might be precluded from holding a driving licence or buying a house, or he might be declared a bankrupt. These are the kind of punishments which also deter because they would be appropriately calculated to fetter a young man's enjoyment of life and some of its rewards while he refuses to honour his responsibilities towards the baby he fathered and forsook.

Such penalties with their social consequences would make it more important, of course, to identify the true father of a bastard. In Denmark it is an offence for an unmarried mother to fail to name all possible fathers. At one time if several men were found to have had intercourse with the woman during the relevant time they were all liable to pay maintenance for the child. The system was abandoned because it was obviously undesirable for a child to find himself with a number of possible fathers; enough to confuse any child, and worse, to lead him to adopt a cynical view of his mother.

Anyway, the increasing reliability of blood tests and anthropological comparisons of the physical features of supposed fathers and their children, outdated the idea of a number of men sharing responsibility for a bastard. The Danes now claim[10] that they succeed in finding the true father in 82 per cent of cases. All men named by the mother are asked to attend for blood tests. They need not submit, but if they do not comply they may be held in custody as material witnesses.

The practice in other Scandinavian countries is similar, but blood tests are still not a compulsory part of the evidence in affiliation cases heard in this country. And this, although it is estimated[11] that comprehensive tests might exonerate more than 75 per cent of men wrongly accused, for blood tests frequently show that the man and the child have relatively uncommon blood factors which the child could not have inherited from the mother.

A blood test may identify a father indirectly by eliminating other suspects. Where a man does not deny intercourse during the material time but says he is not the only possible father, modern tests may lead a man completely to accept a child even though scientifically the evidence is of strong probability rather than certainty of paternity.

Two attempts have been made to introduce compulsory blood tests into England. Both failed. Discussions by a Select Committee were begun in 1938 and interrupted by the war, and it was not until 1961 that an Affiliation Proceedings (Blood Tests) Bill appeared. This did not even receive a first reading in the House of Commons although it would have allowed a court merely to give a direction for tests at the request of the alleged father and to dismiss the application if the mother refused the tests.[12]

Reluctance to accept scientific tests as an aid to determining paternity is not unrelated to widespread attitudes towards bastardy. It would somehow be 'unsporting' of the State to take much initiative in establishing the paternity of a bastard child. Affiliation orders may be won if the woman is persistent enough. The father has simply been proving his manhood in a way which is an accepted ancient tradition. The male seducer is an attractive figure of popular imagination: the seduced are fools, or simply wanton or weak. In the circumstances, inadequate affiliation orders, or the possibility of them, are enough to salve the public conscience.

Abroad, enlightenment goes much further. In Norway the father pays towards the woman's maintenance for three months before the birth and six months after it. The scale of maintenance before the baby's birth is higher than for the rest of the time.

In Denmark the father must help to keep the mother for two months before the birth and one month afterwards. If she falls ill due to her pregnancy or confinement, the payments are extended for up to four months before the birth and nine months after it. The Danish father must pay 25 per cent more for the child's keep during the first two years and so the mother is helped most while the baby's dependency upon her is greatest. In Sweden the father must help to support the mother for six weeks before and after the birth, and for much longer in case of illness.

Under the Polish Family Code of 1950 the father is obliged to make a 'fair contribution' towards the expenses of child-bearing, and to pay a proportion of other 'unavoidable expenses' or even help offset any 'special pecuniary loss'. He must also pay maintenance for three months after the birth and 'for reasons of substance' for longer. Similar measures are enforced in many other countries. Among them are Western Germany, Austria, Switzerland, and Canada. By comparison, what we do in Britain is inadequate and unimaginative. A pregnant woman, married or not, is well provided for by the National Health Service and is able to draw Maternity Benefits.[13] She may also receive further help from charity, and, if she is not working full-time, from social security allowances. Both materially and psychologically, however, it is right to expect the baby's father to pay during her pregnancy and the child's infancy. The sound sense of this is widely recognized by the laws of other countries where much trouble is taken to enforce them. It is no good being humane without being efficient.

Unmarried mothers in Britain are in the 'high risk' category of pregnancies. Fifty years ago over 200 illegitimate children out of every thousand died during their first year: this was more than double the number of legitimate children who died before the age of one.

Happily one of the most dramatic achievements of medicine over the last half century has been the reduction of infant mortality. Even so, the proportion of illegitimate children who die, as against legitimate, remains about the same and is still a matter of great concern.

In the year ending April 1965 the infant mortality rate per thousand live births was 17·5 for legitimate births compared with 28·5 for illegitimate births.[14] In central London (Westminster) which has an illegitimate birth-rate of 18·59 per cent, the infant death-rate is one and a half times the level in legitimate births.[15]

Premature birth is the most prevalent cause of death among babies, but other factors which contribute are poverty, malnutrition, and lack of ante-natal care. The greater loss of illegitimate babies may be explained by the fact that unmarried mothers tend not to make use of the services available to them during their pregnancies. Also they often continue at unsuitable work too long while pregnant and resume work too soon after the baby is born. It must be recognized too, that physical tensions generated by fear and feelings of desolation because of their lover's abandonment can sometimes result in a difficult confinement.

The long-term welfare and happiness of the bastard is rooted in the physical and mental stability of the mother from the early days of pregnancy. The distressing discrepancy in the figures for child deaths among legitimate and illegitimate babies is one of the strongest arguments for bringing English law and practice into line with the best European legislation. Meanwhile it is the voluntary organizations who are most concerned with the role the fathers might play within the rickety framework of Britain's slight legal provisions.

The Salvation Army believes some unmarried fathers suffer a great deal emotionally. Often when young and immature they are liable to run away from the situation out of panic. Certainly, at any one time the 'Army' is looking for 2,000 missing men, both deserting husbands and the fathers of illegitimate children. The head of this branch of the Army's work, Lieut.-Colonel Richard Williams, told me it finds 64 per cent of these men within two or three months.

Nearly every presumed father found by the Salvation Army is willing to take some responsibility. Where there is some proof and he admits paternity, he usually offers between thirty-shillings and two pounds per week to be paid under a private agreement with the 'Army' who forward the money to the mother. In this way the 'Army' keeps a personal interest in some unmarried parents over many years and any special need of the unmarried mother can be brought to the man's attention. Alternatively, the woman can be invited to accept less money if the man has lost his job.

The advantage of these arrangements through a trusted social agency is psychological. According to Lieut.-Col. Williams: 'If police or solicitors or the Ministry of Social Security call at a house with inquiries the ordinary man closes up like a clam. Often we are asked in with the remark, "Seeing it's the Army I might as well tell you. . . ." ' The Salvation Army's experience is confirmed by the work of the Thomas Coram Foundation for Children who also finds that shock often drives unmarried fathers away, but when approached later they are frequently prepared to offer help for the mother and child.

A boy who gives a baby to a girl under sixteen has committed an offence: he may have to go to court, and possibly to prison. Prosecution depends a great deal upon the circumstances and the Church Army finds that when the young people are of much the same age both will be interviewed by the police officers, and frequently the matter rests there.

A study of unmarried fathers under twenty, made by a Church Army social worker, Captain Fred Smith, found 70 per cent admitted paternity and two-thirds offered money. This is a higher proportion than for unmarried fathers as a whole, and Captain Smith attributes this to the relationship many of the young men had with their girl-friends. They were, or felt they were, in love. Also, he points out that they are not as world-wise as older men. Of the fifty young men in Captain Smith's study, six eventually married their girls, and fourteen more would have done so if parents had not intervened. Frequently the anger, arbitrariness, and bad advice of parents make the situation worse. Some even insist that the young father denies paternity, quite regardless of the quality of the relationship between the couple and what such a denial will mean to them.

Those mother and baby homes which will not allow unmarried fathers to visit the mothers and their babies are adopting an equally misguided semi-parental attitude although, of course, most of these homes are voluntary institutions and are entitled to make their own rules. These barriers go up at a crucial time, when the

E

parents, particularly if they are young, are feeling much closer together and are in grievous need of each other's support.

Maybe one of the reasons why 'homes' often insist upon shutting out unmarried fathers is the new status they have achieved under fairly recent legislation. It is too easy now for the father of a bastard to appear to be a threat to the successful adoption of the child.

Under the Adoption Act of 1958 the father has merely the right to be heard during adoption proceedings. The Legitimacy Act of 1959, however, provides for confusion by allowing fathers the right to sue for custody. So any adoption may be blocked by the father offering his child a home himself.[16]

The law is also infuriatingly ambiguous. Under the 1958 Act the guardian *ad litem*, who has legal custody of the child until its adoption, has 'to inform the court if he *learns* of any person, claiming to be the father, who wishes to be heard by the court on the question of whether an adoption order should be made'. There is no clear direction that the father should be found and asked point-blank if he wishes to be heard.

The muddle of existing legislation is made worse by the differing attitudes of the courts. Some magistrates and judges prefer that the father's views be made known in all cases where he has been named. Others only where the father has paid towards the child's upkeep. Some courts make no particular demands for information concerning the father. Adoption societies, however, are increasingly anxious to obtain some form of consent from the father because, while this is not legally required, he can, nevertheless, effectively challenge the adoption. He might have many motives for doing so. He may love his child and be able to offer a suitable home. He may hope to force marriage with the mother, or merely wish to hinder the adoption out of pique. Again, he may have genuine doubts about adoption.

Common sense demands that the law should direct reasonable efforts to be made to discover the father's views and intentions. When a father wishes to exercise his custody rights the case should be heard without delay, preferably before the child goes to adopters. Adopters, already concerned about the prospect of the natural mother changing her mind and wanting her baby back, should not also have to worry about the father unexpectedly challenging the adoption.

Sometimes mothers do not want the father to be found, and may even refuse to give his name. The adoption society, however, has responsibilities towards its adopters and, more importantly, to the child who has a psychological need to know who fathered him. Adoption agencies need background information about both the father and the mother, and this can only be reliable when it comes from the man himself.

These illustrations[17] show how wrong the girl can be about her lover. One man said to be Spanish, or perhaps Persian, turned out to be Russian. A 'University student' was an engineer who had just completed a month's extra-mural course at university. A 'wealthy' student with a supposed income of £20 per week, was found to be living on a grant of under £36 per month. A 'single' man promising marriage was a married man with a long history of mental illness. Another man, described as having a brother with 'mental trouble', was found merely to have had a brother backward at school.

NOTES

1. Schofield, Michael: *Sexual Behaviour of Young People* (Longmans, Green, 1965).

2. 1,837 young people, aged from fifteen to nineteen, were interviewed, half boys and half girls, chosen from a random sample of seven areas in England and Wales.

3. A sociological study of the mothers in a Midland city (disguised as 'Midborough') who had babies in 1949, made by Valerie Hughes of the London School of Economics 1950.

4. Exceptions are if the man has gone abroad; if she has evidence that he has at some time contributed towards the child's support; or if the case is brought by the National Assistance Board or the Local authority.

5. Affiliation Orders Act 1914, Sec. 7.

6. 'Fatherless by Law?' A study by the Board for Social Responsibility of the National Assembly of the Church of England (Church Information Office, 1966).

7. Wimperis, Virginia, *The Unmarried Mother and Her Child* (George Allen & Unwin Ltd., 1960).

8. Of course, no further arrears accrue while a man is in prison. Also the

Courts may wipe out existing arrears on review of a committal. If this is likely then the mother should be told and may attend the review proceedings.

9. 1954 report of the legal sub-committee of the National Council for the Unmarried Mother and Her Child. The Committee by a majority decided to support the scheme, despite the supposed difficulties, because it would clearly avert much hardship.

10. An address given at the annual meeting of the National Council for the Unmarried Mother and Her Child, July 1965, by Professor Leonard Schapiro.

11. Appendix 4 in 'Fatherless by Law' (Church Information Office, 1966). A note compiled from information supplied by Dr. Alan Grant, lecturer in Forensic Serology at Guy's Hospital, London.

12. In May 1968 the Court of Appeal ruled that the paternity of a boy of three could be decided by a blood test, after assurance that the result would be conclusive. Lord Denning, Master of the Rolls, said: 'The object of the court always is to ascertain the truth. And when in these days of scientific advance we have the means available we should not hesitate to use them whenever the occasion requires.'

13. An unmarried mother may claim the maternity benefits if she is herself insured and has paid the necessary number of contributions. The benefits are: Maternity Grant, an outright payment of £22; Maternity allowance of £4 a week normally paid for eighteen weeks beginning eleven weeks before the baby is expected but not for any time of paid work.

14. An investigation carried out jointly by the Social Medicine Research Unit of the Medical Research Council and the General Register Office.

15. *Daily Telegraph*, 4 February 1967.

16. A much-publicized example is the 'blood-tie case': In Re C. (an infant), Court of Appeal, 21 February 1966. The child was taken away from prospective adopters at seventeen months. Two of the three judges contended the infant would lose an important factor in the development of his personality if he were not brought up by his natural father. (See page 23.)

17. A paper prepared by Captain Fred Smith of the Church Army for the Chichester Diocesan Moral Welfare Association, 'The Putative Father and Adoption', 1967.

4

Adopted Children

THERE has been considerable research during the past twenty years into adoption practice, but more questions have been provoked by it than answered. Much of the evidence is inconclusive, or worse, contradictory. The main conclusion that emerges from the endeavours of all the researchers could have been reached by common sense: 'That no other circumstance of adoption is as important as the kind of people the adopters are and the kind of home they create.'[1]

In other words, although it may be that adopted children are beset with more difficulties in growing up, it is the capacity of the parents which is of paramount importance, and it is the good parents who will succeed with any child, adopted or not, and the bad parents who will fail.

Although this research conclusion may appear obvious and banal, it has probably contributed to a change in adoption practice over the years from an emphasis on the thorough assessment of babies to a more careful selection of adopters.

In all the volume of research some important questions have never been investigated and others have been wrongly raised because they defy definition. Attempts to establish a 'success rate' for adoptions are meaningless and the results, often misinterpreted, encourage dangerously false ideas that most adopted children are maladjusted.

What is meant by success or failure in adoption? When are these judgements to be made? At school age, adolescence, or maturity?

Apart from the extreme cases when application is made for a child to be re-adopted,[2] which must be tantamount to failure, what are the researchers' yardsticks? The question of 'success' is rarely raised about ordinary families, and it seems pointless to pose it about adopting families. Is the evidence to be found solely in the numbers of adopted children before the courts, or sent to Approved Schools, or child guidance clinics, or psychiatrists' consulting rooms? There are obvious shortcomings about studying only the adopted children in difficulties.

There is no doubt that a greater number of adopted children are receiving psychiatric treatment in both Britain and America. In this country it has been estimated[3] that the proportion of adoptive families referred for psychiatric advice is more than double that for the population as a whole. The proportion of adopted children in residential schools for the maladjusted may be three times greater than the national percentage if one research study is a good pointer.[4]

The incidence of adopted children seen by psychiatrists is impressive, but it does not tell anything about the mental health and happiness of those not having treatment. If any worth-while conclusions are to be drawn, other studies are needed to show the proportion of adopted children successfully adjusted to life.

Statistics in these areas are also deservedly suspect because of the predisposition of parents, if only subconsciously, to blame adoption when difficulties arise, as inevitably they will. Most children go through phases when they steal, lie, destroy, and are over-aggressive. It is too easy for adopters to attribute these unwelcome aspects of growing-up to an 'heredity' for which they have no responsibility. Often, they are also encouraged in over-anxious attitudes by doctors and psychiatrists too ready to seize upon adoption as the root cause of any trouble from the child. In short, much intellectual theorizing about adoption over-emphasizes the vulnerability of adopted children and creates a climate in which difficulties are expected almost as a matter of course.

A number of circumstances suggest this vulnerability.[5] Most adopted children are illegitimate and carried by mothers whose personal and family life are likely to be beset by problems: pregnancy stress, physical and emotional, can have adverse effects even while the baby is still in the womb. Infants are sensitive to emotion and strain, and the adopted child is likely to be exposed in the early months to both the grief of the mother and the insecurity of the adopters. There is still widespread and deep-seated disapproval towards bastardy in our society, and the fact that adoptive families are a minority group is another aspect that has not been systematically explored.

At last more broadly based research projects are going on. The Home Office Research Unit is surveying more than a thousand cases of adoption for more detailed information, and the National Bureau for Co-operation in Child Care, with Home Office help, is also studying a random sample of seven-year-olds adopted in Britain. One or both parents will be interviewed and the children's development and progress explored in relation to their adoption history and present home background.

An important object of the research is to discover what effects, if any, different methods of adoption have upon the children and their parents. The Bureau is also making a critical survey of research literature about the care of children for the Home Office. This review will cover research into adoption, foster care, residential care, and the administration of the social services for children during the past fifteen years or so in Britain, Western Europe, America, and Israel.[6]

These research efforts are to be welcomed particularly in this country where adoption procedures remain dominated by the amateur tradition. The most casual of these procedures are adoptions arranged by 'third parties'—anyone who is prepared to act as a go-between for the unmarried mother and to introduce her baby to prospective adopters. Of course, the degree of care taken in placing the baby varies enormously, much depending upon the people involved. Sometimes the baby is placed directly by the mother, or adopted by relatives. Again, the 'third party' may be a doctor placing patients' babies with childless couples among medical colleagues. On the other hand, a 'third party' may be an acquaintance from the public house or launderette.

It is astonishing that at the time of writing no official figures for the number of 'third party' adoptions in Britain are available. There is, however, good evidence to suggest that it is quite a common practice and as the issues it raises are of such importance they will be examined in the next chapter.

Other adoptions are arranged by some eighty-five local authorities (local councils may choose whether to engage in adoption work) and by about seventy voluntary societies, either exclusively or as a part of their charitable work. The largest group consists of twenty-eight societies which developed out of Church of England Moral Welfare Work. Next are twenty-four societies which are primarily children's welfare agencies, with adoption only one of a variety of services. There are seven national societies providing only adoption services, three of them tied to a Church. Most of the remaining thirteen have developed from local council or social service.

No common standards exist, and in Britain adoption agencies are criticized rightly, wrongly, and variously. Some are attacked for making too rigorous and unrealistic demands upon adopters; others for a comparatively careless approach to prospective parents. Each society imposes different requirements and these reveal its peculiar prejudices and differences of emphases.

The agencies largely follow their own idiosyncrasies when choosing adopters. One of few common requirements by law is that the baby must be placed with adopters of the religion specified by the mother.[7] When a mother surrenders her baby for adoption she rarely denies any religion. This may sometimes be on grounds of expediency: many of the voluntary societies are Church-founded and she does not wish to offend those who she hopes will help her. Far more often it is likely that while having no religious convictions herself she wants religion for her child as a source of goodness and comfort, as a talisman. In this increasingly secular country, where the majority of adults are now unbelievers, there is still a potent conviction that children need religion for their proper upbringing. A Gallup Poll in 1966[8] showed that only 4 per cent of those interviewed are opposed to religion in schools.

Unlike the voluntary societies those local authorities who arrange adoptions have no need to find religious adopters unless the mother makes this stipulation when completing the consent form. But often they appoint a supervising committee which has the same rigid outlook as the societies over religious beliefs. Obviously, Christians are not the only people capable of giving an insecure child the love and care he needs. There are many loving and mature parents who acknowledge no religious convictions. Some children may suffer if placed in a religious home where the outlooks are too harsh and narrow. What would appear to be an un-Christian denial of love is insistence upon a specifically religious home for a child when the alternative is life in an institution. There the child may no doubt acquire a formal religious training but one without roots in his own experience. The idea of a loving Heavenly Father stems from the experience of the love and care of a human father, and to a large extent human parents establish the pattern for the ideas of God formed and kept by the young child.

But this is not essentially an issue of religious bigotry. The real arbiter in the situation is the child's mother to whom Parliament has given the unqualified right of naming her child's religion when she signs consent to adoption. The trouble is that she may be unaware of the importance of this stipulation and what may seem no more than a formality can prejudice the baby's chances of a speedy adoption. The position must be made abundantly clear to the mother, particularly if there is a shortage of adopters. The consent form should be redesigned to ask the mother whether she would agree to adopters of any other denominations apart from the one she has named; and if no suitable adopters of the stipulated religion can be found whether the child should be placed with non-religious parents. She could also be invited to stipulate that special arrangements be made for the child's religious education if this need arises.

In this way some of the difficulties inherent in the present situation would be overcome. It must be remembered that many mothers are only nominally religious and would be equally content for their child to be brought up an Anglican or, say, a Baptist. Acknowledgement of the vagueness of most people's religious feelings today would facilitate closer co-operation between adoption agencies, widen the scope for selection of adopters and help to ensure that adherence to the letter of the law did not deny a child a real home. The law requires that one adopter must be at least twenty-five and the other twenty-one years old, although many young couples have their own children before this age and make excellent parents. Most adoption agencies fix upper age limits while a few are prepared to be more flexible. Forty is frequently the age limit for the wife who wishes to adopt an infant. It is considered sensible to exclude adopters beyond normal child-bearing age so that their children correspond more closely to the natural family. The theory is that the difficult years of adolescence are likely to over-tax elderly parents, and there is always an increased danger that such parents may die before the child has grown up.

In many other countries, however, adoption is only open to middle-aged couples.[9] In Greece and Germany (with special provisions) no one under fifty may adopt a child. The same rule applied in Italy until 1967. In Spain forty-five is the minimum age; in Austria, France, and Switzerland it is forty. Only Scandinavia has similar age requirements to British agencies. In this country there is no maximum age fixed for adopters by law, and third-party adoptions are often arranged for older couples turned down by the registered societies.

Some societies demand flawless health records; others seem unduly concerned with material considerations of housing and income. More importantly, many societies appear obsessively anxious there should be no likelihood of adopters having a child of their own later and so evidence of infertility is required. This requirement caused a fuss in Lewisham recently when it was alleged that the Council was breaking the law in imposing fertility tests.[10] The Adoption Act doesn't require adopters to produce this kind of evidence; on the other hand, it allows the agencies the freedom to make their own rules about such matters. The fear is clearly that a natural child would be treated differently and loved more than his adopted brothers or sisters. The suspicion reveals a poor opinion of the adopters' capacities to love and cherish the babies entrusted to them and ignores the fact that often the adopted child is the forerunner of a natural family.

Justly or unjustly, the adoption society is popularly seen as a busybodying agency preoccupied with delaying tactics. Many couples are intimidated by the prospect of going through 'all the rigmarole' and this partly explains why the societies do not receive as many applications as they would like from the working class.

More sophisticated couples are often bemused by the naïvety and tortured thinking of many earnest social workers. Great emphasis is laid in modern adoption work upon a couple's reasons and there are a host of undesirable motives. Children must not be wanted as 'companions' or 'status symbols', or to allay feelings of inadequacy and mortality. Just such reasons, of course, activate many parents of natural children, and they are often none the worse mothers and fathers because of their human fears and weaknesses.

What is the textbook answer of the nervous prospective mother to the social workers' critical inquiry: 'Why do you want to adopt a baby?' She might say: 'We've always wanted children and we're very upset we haven't had one of our own.' Thinks the caseworker: 'Has this couple really accepted the fact of their own infertility?' Or: 'Our married life doesn't seem right without children—after all, a child makes a home.' Thinks the caseworker: 'Is the child wanted as a cure for neurosis or marital problems?' Or: the would-be mother may appear dangerously ingenuous: 'It's quite simple, we love children.' Thinks the caseworker: 'Are they over-senti-mentalizing? Are they nursing romantic fantasies likely to be ruptured by the practical everyday demands of a child?'

The experienced social worker endowed with common sense and kindness, should be able to see behind the anxious words, the awkward manner, and to make good judgements. The natural desire of the prospective adopters to make a good impression often betrays them into creating the worst impression. But selection methods can become over-sophisticated and in clever sifting of motives the social worker may overlook the real characters of the people she is interviewing. Adoption societies looking for utopian parents forget that few natural parents would pass the stringent tests they often impose and they rarely make any allowance for the contribution the baby will make to the *parents'* development.

Many couples who wish to adopt turn to third parties because of the comparative speed and simplicity of the preliminaries. Also, naturally and rightly, they want a baby as soon as possible after he is born. Many adoption societies will not place a baby until he is six weeks old, the lowest age at which the mother can give her formal consent. The baby may be placed with prospective adopters earlier (by the child being viewed as a foster-child until he is six weeks old) and, of course, the mother may lawfully change her mind any time before the signing of the Court adoption order.

She has, in fact, to give her formal consent on a number of occasions, so multiplying her emotional suffering. At present she gives a preliminary consent to the adoption agency, formal consent before a J.P., corroboration of consent to a guardian *ad litem*, and finally gets a notice of hearing asking if she wants to object.[11] Once the prospective parents have lodged their papers for an adoption order (they can do so any time after the baby is six weeks old) the mother no longer has an automatic right to have her baby back if she changes her mind. She may now have to dispute the case in court.

More societies now place babies for adoption much earlier than used to be their practice, in a bid to beat the third parties, but many agencies still favour three to four months, or later in cases where they are uncertain of the child's inheritance and potential development. There is little evidence to suggest that a child's development can be more accurately forecast after a few months of life than a few weeks.

On the other hand, much research suggests young babies can be seriously harmed by lack of mothering and if continuity of care in early infancy is broken. A baby's world is his mother. He will accept a substitute but he needs her immediately: delay is damaging.

Dr. John Bowlby writes: 'There is a very serious danger that keeping a baby in a nursery awaiting adoption in the belief that in a few more months an accurate prediction can be made will itself produce retardation, which is then taken as evidence that the baby is inherently backward. So there develops the paradoxical situation in which misguided caution in arranging adoption creates a baby who at first appears and ultimately becomes unfitted for it.'[12]

A mother for the baby must not be postponed: or he becomes sick with 'institutionalization'. The disease numbs the emotions and fetters the intelligence. Its worst victims become unloving and unlovable.

It is sometimes claimed that local authorities take up more professional attitudes towards problems of adoption. They are said to be less doctrinaire and more modern in their methods. The truth is that many workers for both statutory and voluntary organizations are untrained and the implications of this are impossible to discover because of the wide variety of adoption arrangements and the lack of research into the subject.

In fact, investigation into almost any aspect of adoption in England is hampered by official vagueness and lack of information. Even the percentage for the number of adopted children in the population is only a rough approximation. Figures for England range from 1·3 per cent to 2 per cent. These variations are partly due to the relatively recent origin of adoption statistics and to the variety of techniques used to obtain an estimate of adopted children. Also in some calculations children adopted by their own mothers are excluded.[13] Little effort has been made to analyse the meagre statistics which are available about the more than half million adoptions legalized since 1926.[14] In 1966 the number of children adopted was 22,792—11,616 boys and 11,176 girls. Of the total, 4,912 were legitimate and 17,880 illegitimate. But the figures do not reveal how many relatives adopt children, only whether the adopter is a parent or not. Five fathers adopted their illegitimate children and ninety mothers did so. The ages and sexes of adopted children are recorded (about 25 per cent are under six months when the adoption goes through), and so are figures of adoption orders made in the High Court (50), county courts (14,880) and juvenile courts (7,862). No breakdown is given about numbers of adoptions arranged through third parties, voluntary societies, and local authorities. It is not possible to find out how many coloured or handicapped children are adopted, or remain available for adoption. Also unrecorded are those mothers who reclaim their babies before adoption is complete, and how many adopters themselves return babies during the probationary three months. Applications from would-be adopters are unregistered. There are no figures of those who want to adopt but are turned down, nor of mothers who offer children to adoption agencies and are turned away. Finally, there is no way to discover the most important figure of all: how many children are awaiting adoption and how many people have been approved to adopt.

Not only are the few statistics which are available from the Home Office inadequate, they are so poorly presented as to defy further useful breakdown. Attempts to gain more information receive polite rebuffs.

Miss Alice Bacon, Minister of State at the Home Office, was asked in Parliament on 26 July 1965, to reveal the ratio of children available to adopters coming forward. In reply she gave only figures of children going out of care because they were adopted. This was not the question put to her.

One is told that this crucial matter of the ratio of adopters to babies is hard for 'outsiders' to understand. So much depends apparently on suitability—the suitability of the adopters offering homes, the suitability of the babies to occupy them, and whether there are enough caseworkers with enough facilities to arrange it all.

The Home Office in correspondence said no 'precise' information about the percentage of adoptions arranged by 'third parties' was available. Certainly they gave none at all. They also offered no figures of coloured children in institutions. Asked to estimate the supply and demand position of children and adopters, the Home Office replied this could not be accurately assessed 'although present indications seem to be that the gap between the two is narrowing'.[15]

For some years now these 'present indications' have been concerning the social agencies. They have begun to ask if some of their hard and fast rules (easy to apply while would-be adopters outnumbered available babies by ten to one) will survive if the supply of adopters dries up. The questioning may become academic if potential adopters are so few that more unmarried mothers determined to place their babies turn to third-party arrangements.

The National Council for the Unmarried Mother and Her Child says[16] social workers sometimes find it difficult now to arrange adoptions in the south, south-west, and some parts of the north. Everywhere boys are harder to place than girls and homes open to babies of mixed parentage are rare.

The Standing Conference of Societies Registered for Adoption recently reported[17] that fourteen agencies as well as most of the nineteen Roman Catholic societies want more applicants. A few are experiencing real difficulties and many tell of trouble in placing baby boys of limited potentialities. To some extent shortages of adopters are associated with rules about church membership but one of the societies most in need is not tied to a Church. Even the Church societies are now less rigid and only six of them insist that applicants attend church regularly.

Many societies and local authorities give some information of this sort in specialized journals; but the wider picture is unrevealed because of the different policies and procedures of adoption agencies. Often an admission committee deals with children in need of care while an adoption committee takes only those children who appear easy to place. Only about half the voluntary societies accept children with anything more than a minor handicap of health or background. Fewer still place any significant number of coloured children.[18]

The Church of England Children's Society has reduced adoption work because its child-care workers are so busy with foster-parents and catering for the needs of older children out to work. It should be remembered many adoption organizations are also involved in a wide range of welfare work, often in co-operation with the local authorities. Some offer considerable service to unmarried mothers and much further effort is devoted to families in difficulties.

Lack of nursery space or too few short-term foster mothers may both affect adoption opportunities as well as the shortage of skilled caseworkers. Much nursery accommodation is taken up by children whose mothers do not wish them to be adopted but who may or may not manage to find suitable homes of their own in which to care for their children. It is also apparent that many voluntary societies are short of money and loath to ask for it.

All this means that when a particular society says it is 'over-subscribed' with adopters the term can be completely misleading for there is no way of knowing how many babies needing parents have had to be turned away. No one can quarrel with the practical good sense of these voluntary organizations which confine their charity within limits they can handle competently. Unfortunately an awareness of limitations does not always bring an accompanying desire to get rid of them. In 1965 the five principal voluntary organizations for children's welfare accepted less than one in four of the babies they were asked to take into their care (this did not include babies accepted for adoption nor those who went to them on payment from local authorities).[19] The main reasons were lack of space in nurseries or of suitable foster-homes. In a high proportion of cases the mothers wished their babies adopted. When they were refused the opportunity for adoption it was for three main reasons: the baby's mental or physical handicap; an adverse family heredity; or his colour.[20] In general it is the children of poor inheritance or who are regarded as subnormal physically or mentally who are most difficult to get on to the adoption lists of agencies. This in spite of a Government committee report condemning any discouragement of adoption of handicapped children.[21]

There are other disturbing reasons, even less welcome. The Western National Adoption Society reported in 1965 *Child Adoption* No. 47, that twenty-seven babies were refused by them mainly 'because of the irregular and immoral life of the mother'.

Clearly there are real difficulties in finding enough adopters for children who are 'hard to place' because of age or handicap but I am certain that 'the unadoptable child' is often the forlorn creation of misguided professionalism. These children are too often forgotten when public assurances are given that there are more than enough prospective adopters. Too frequently only children officially 'suitable for adoption' are counted, and the plight of those children in the greatest need overlooked. These unfortunate children are frequently doubly handicapped, the deprivation of parents' love added to their existing burdens.

The practical problems involved in placing handicapped and under-privileged children with adopters are often small in comparison with the difficulties of changing entrenched attitudes. Here, according to one recent investigator,[22] committee members, doctors, matrons, and house-parents are often more obsessed than social workers with the idea of gilt-edged babies and the need to protect adoptive parents. 'We shall only begin to find enough homes when we change our attitudes and instead of saying of exceptionally good applicants "we must find them a superior baby" say instead "which of our needy children could they help most?" '

NOTES

1. Pringle Kellmer, M. L., *Adoption—Facts and Fallacies* (Longmans, Green in association with the National Bureau for Co-operation in Child Care, 1967).

2. This is a process permitted by the last two Adoption Acts.

3. Humphrey, M. and Ounsted, C., 'Adoptive families referred for psychiatric advice: *The Children, British Journal of Psychiatry*, Part 1, 1963, p. 109.

4. Pringle Kellmer, M. L., 'The incidence of some supposedly adverse family conditions and of left-handedness in schools for maladjusted children', *Brit. J. Ed. Psch. 31*, Part 2, 1961.

5. Pringle Kellmer, M. L., *Adoption—Facts and Fallacies* (Longmans, Green in association with the National Bureau for Co-operation in Child Care, 1967).

6. The first in this series was published last year (1967)—*Adoption—Facts and Fallacies*—offering an admirable review of research in the United States, Canada, and Great Britain between 1948 and 1965. There were only three large-scale studies, all of them American. During these seventeen years only about a dozen studies were completed and published in this country, although there are now almost as many projects under way in Britain (18) as there are in Canada and America together (21). Other titles in this series are also now published.

7. The Agnostics Adoption Society was founded 1963/4 to help prospective adopters for whom there had been no adequate provision before. These included agnostics, non-practising Christians, couples of mixed religion, Jewish couples, and couples who have been involved in divorces. But the society has only one caseworker (due to shortage of funds) and is not yet arranging many adoptions, nine in 1966.

8. Social Surveys (Gallup Poll) Ltd. Investigation into the religious and moral attitudes of the English. This was carried out for ABC Television, 1963/4.

9. This requirement may well be a legacy from earlier times when adoption

F

was only considered as a last resort for families faced with extinction due to lack of progeny.

10. *Daily Telegraph* report, 6 February 1967.

11. In many American states and in some European countries the mother may assign her parental right by deed to the adoption society and she would take no further part in the proceedings.

In Australia an unmarried mother rarely sees her baby; the practice in England is regarded as 'refined torture'.

12. Bowlby, John: 'Maternal Care and Mental Health', 1951. A report prepared on behalf of the World Health Organisation as a contribution to the United Nations programme for the welfare of homeless children. This brilliant report provided a strong stimulus to productive research and improved services for deprived children in many countries, although a vast amount remains to be done.

13. Pringle Kellmer, M. L., *Adoption—Facts and Fallacies* (Longmans, Green in association with the National Bureau for Co-operation in Child Care 1967).

14. The first Adoption Act 1926. The following year 3,000 children were adopted.

15. Letter to author, 17 November 1966.

16. N.C.U.M.C. Annual Report, April 1965–March 1966.

17. *Child Adoption No. 51*, 1967. Article by Jane Rowe, adviser and tutor to the Standing Conference.

18. *Child Adoption No. 51*, 1967. Jane Rowe on 'Present Standards and Future Needs'.

19. *Child Care News*, September 1966, gave the figures: 821 babies accepted into care by the five societies, and 2,494 turned away. The Societies were: Children's Society; Crusade of Rescue; Dr. Barnardo's; National Children's Homes; and Thomas Coram Foundation for Children.

20. Babies considered 'unsuitable' for adoption were suffering from such handicaps as congenital heart defect, cleft palate and hare lip, hydrocephalus, severe kidney damage, physical abnormality, mental subnormality, progressive disease or severe prematurity. 'Many of the babies' mothers were unstable or of subnormal intelligence. Some were living on their own with no family support, others came from broken homes.'

21. Report of the Departmental Committee on the Adoption of Children, Cmnd. 9248 (H.M.S.O., 1954), known as the Hurst Committee after its chairman.

22. Rowe, Jane, *Parents, Children and Adoption* (Routledge & Kegan Paul, 1966).

5

Third-Party Adoptions

MANY adoption societies were founded to prevent exploitation of unmarried mothers and to curb the activities of those profiting from a black-market in babies. Even today it is claimed that unwanted babies in this country can be bought and sold.

Such allegations make good newspaper copy. The reports speak of unnamed private nursing homes where adoptions as well as confinements are catered for at considerable expense to the unmarried mothers, or the adopters, or both parties. What is always missing from these accounts is reliable evidence.

Obviously, it is difficult to establish the facts about nefarious transactions. Those involved fear publicity or prosecution. The difficulties are increased, however, by governmental reluctance to publish what is known.

In the House of Commons on 11 December 1964, Mr. Leo Abse, Labour M.P. for Pontypool, questioned the Attorney-General on the subject. He asked if anything would be done to stop illicit trade in babies. He also wanted to know how many prosecutions had been brought under adoption law during the past five years. The Attorney-General replied that this information was 'not available'; but he added he had no evidence which would justify legal proceedings in connection with adoptions arranged by private nursing homes.

This parliamentary exchange followed a series of articles about private adoptions in the *Daily Mail*, which in turn was stimulated by a conference of the National Council of Women where there was a demand for tighter legal control of third-party arrangements. One unidentified interviewee of the *Daily Mail* was: 'A thirty-nine-year old business woman who, after trying unsuccessfully to adopt through the recognized channels, was offered a baby by a doctor for £200.' Also mentioned was a 'solicitor in Yorkshire' whose fees for finding a baby were alleged to be £300.

Another national conference, this time of Labour women in 1965, was told by Mrs. Eileen White: 'London is the centre of a growing and appalling traffic in babies.' More newspaper articles and further fruitless questioning in Parliament followed.

It has also been said in recent years that babies are taken from England to Ireland and sold there 'for export'. A deputy in the *Dail*, Maureen O'Connell, is on record[1] as saying that a total of 523 children were sent to America in three years.

It may well be that baby marketing flourishes in other parts of the world, particularly America, where the demand is unusually high and the requirements of adoption agencies onerous to meet. The market price for an illegitimate baby in the United States has been estimated at one thousand pounds.

In Greece, however, where there is much poverty, many children apparently are sold for a pittance.[2] The Ministry of the Interior grew suspicious of the large number of emigration visas for infants. Many were submitted by one person, and one Greek lawyer was found to have been proxy for the adoption of about a thousand Greek babies by foreign couples. A baby was recently sold by his parents to a stranger in Athens for £17, the sum they needed to obtain emigration papers to West Germany. There are moves to strengthen Greek adoption laws to stop this despicable traffic.

The black-market in babies was acknowledged by Dr. John Bowlby in his report for the United Nations in 1951. He wrote then: 'It is a social and legal problem which one day will require attention, but it would be foolish to tackle so thorny a problem before the recognized machinery for adoption is in the hands of qualified people who can be relied upon to make realistic assessments of prospective parents. This will take time.'

The proportions of the problem remain unknown. Certainly, in this country few cases of commercial dealings in babies reach the police courts today. A legacy of deep suspicion was created in Barnardo's time when unwanted children were bartered, sold, and re-sold, and sometimes systematically starved to death for the insurance money. Current fears of widespread business dealings in British babies may derive more from folklore than from fact, but no doubt they still influence the sensitivities of all those engaged in working with homeless children.

It is a striking fact that third-party adoptions are abhorrent to professionals although there is scant evidence to support their disapproval. The inadequacy, or total absence, of casework in third-party adoptions may be regretted. On the other hand, they achieve an immediacy unequalled and unwanted by the reputable societies, which are sometimes said to be more concerned to delay adoptions than to arrange them.

Moreover, if third parties did not act, the registered agencies as they are now organized could not meet the national need. They have neither sufficient workers nor resources for their existing commitments.

Third parties may organize 40 per cent of all adoptions, a quarter of them 'within the family'. No official figures are available, for the Home Office appears to regard them as secret or unimportant. In the circumstances the best source is the Standing Conference of Societies Registered for Adoption whose tutor gave me these estimates[3] showing how the 40 per cent figure for third-party adoptions is calculated: 25 per cent adopted by relatives (often mother and step-father); 10 per cent placed direct by the mother; 5 per cent other 'third parties'.

Apart from the mothers who themselves place their babies, third parties are simply private individuals trying to help, although a few may spend a great deal of time arranging many adoptions. The classic example of the busy third party is the gynaecologist whose patients include women anxious to dispose of their babies and other women longing to have them. Some third parties with these opportunities will arrange more adoptions in a year than the smaller registered agencies find possible.[4] These regularly called upon third parties are often well known for their scrupulous concern for the good of all involved.

Others are regarded with wariness and suspicion because of the methods they employ and the scale of their work. A few use printed forms which create a false impression that they are approved adoption organisations, or they may offer misleading assurances that they are working in conjunction with the welfare authorities. This claim rests on the fact that the local authorities, to whom they must give fourteen days' notice before a child goes to the prospective adopters, have not actually forbidden the child's reception.

In third-party adoption both the third party and the would-be parents need to tell the local council a fortnight before they take the child so that a caseworker can make inquiries. If the report on the home is bad, the local authority can prohibit the child's reception; but this rarely happens. There is the problem of what to do with the baby. He is kept from the love awaiting him and has to suffer further separations, going into a residential nursery or foster home. He may also become the object of a legal struggle, for the prospective adopters have a right of appeal for his delivery to their home.[5]

The caseworker who feels dissatisfied with the third-party arrangement is more likely to allow the child's reception, and to shift the responsibility for a realistic assessment on to the guardian *ad litem*. It is the court, with whom the application papers are lodged, who appoints the child's guardian *ad litem*, to act until an adoption order is made. Usually, the local children's officer or his representative is appointed, but if the council arranged the adoption then it is recommended someone entirely unconnected with the arrangements should be appointed, such as a probation officer or some other trained social worker. If the guardian *ad litem* reports adversely to the court upon a third-party adoption it is likely the order will be refused. In this case, however, there is nothing to prevent the child remaining in the same home unless it can be proved that the child's health or well-being is endangered when the local authority may apply for an order to remove him.

Witnesses told the Hurst Committee[6] that little use has ever been made of this power because of the difficulty of getting convincing evidence. The safeguard appears to be effective only if the material conditions are exceptionally unsatisfactory, or the custodian of the child grossly unsuitable. So if an adoption order is refused it is probable that the child stays where he is, under supervision but without secure status. For these reasons a guardian *ad litem* may be loath to criticize the home, and courts tend to make an adoption order even if the arrangement is not a particularly satisfactory one.

If an adoption order is refused when the arrangements are made by a voluntary society or local authority, the child must be returned to the agency within seven days, and if the prospective parents are unreasonably dilatory in applying for an adoption order the agency may remove him. The law does not require a registered society or its adopters to tell the local authority *before* the child's reception. Casework has already been carried out. The couple must inform the authority when they have the baby of their intention to adopt, and the three months' probationary period begins from the date they notify, so long as the baby is at least six weeks' old.

They will be visited by a worker from the adoption society and a child-care officer from the local authority who will be supervising. It has been argued with some cogency that the local authority caseworker represents an unnecessary multiplication of effort, particularly as the guardian *ad litem*, usually another official of the local authority, will also be making inquiries once application papers have been filed with the court.

Another hazard which threatens the third-party adoption is that in some cases the arrangement may be local and known, and lack any protection from the privacy of secrecy or distance. There is also risk when only one marriage partner wants to adopt. It is possible to arrange the adoption through a third party and to present the other partner with a baby: instant parenthood, without the tedium of lengthy preliminaries, or the opportunities for joint consultation and action. The marriage partner carrying out this stratagem may alone notify the local authority of the baby's forthcoming arrival, or ignore the statutory notice and plead ignorance of the law. In these circumstances a prosecution is seldom brought, and the baby stays. It is the blackmail of *fait accompli*.

It may well be asked why third-party adoptions are legally permitted considering the potential dangers, but much can be put forward on the credit side for both children and adopters. Leaving aside ruthless third parties who place babies for financial gain, most personal arrangements are prompted by neighbourly good-will and genuine affection for the child and his family.

The Hurst Committee[7] pointed out that the courts are familiar with adopters who are friends of the mother, fellow-workers, or landladies who have grown to love a child entrusted to their care. 'Such people, although their income may be small and their housing conditions cramped, are prompted by the highest motives and are prepared to accept the child as he is and incorporate him into their family although they would never have set out to seek a child for adoption in the ordinary way.'

It is also likely that any restrictions on third-party adoptions would merely drive the practice underground. The arrangements would be the same but adopters would not apply for adoption orders.

Again, some adopters set their hearts upon a particular child, rather than one chosen for them by others, however competent. The reasons for their choice may defy analysis. Nevertheless, they can be compelling and cause them to accept a child more completely, 'for better, for worse', just because he is their own choice.

A common reason for delaying adoptions is for considerations of health, the health both of the two sets of parents and particularly of the child, but there can be little justification for postponing adoption for the sake of medical diagnosis. So many illnesses can now be cured, so many handicaps lightened, that it seems a pessimistic folly to deny a child the benefits of an early adoption on uncertain health grounds.

Few people will rebuff a child who is not robust: this will often bring them closer together. Acceptance of health problems by parents who have adopted young babies is natural. It is their responsibility and is accepted automatically. Many adopters not only often show a preference for an 'unattractive' child, instead of a 'beautiful' one, but frequently continue with the legal adoption of a child who during probation has developed some serious illness or disability.[8]

Even mental backwardness, which most people find difficult to accept, calls forth from some adopters an extraordinary love and patience if they have identified with the child young enough. And, so far as mental development is concerned, it appears that tests in infancy are useless in forecasting school-age abilities.[9] It is generally recognized that probably the best indication of potential intelligence is the intelligence of the parents; although this can be no more than a rough guide and adoptive parents, like natural parents, must be prepared to take a normal biological risk. Most parents, anyway, are not concerned with having intelligent children. They want a loving one, and this can best be achieved by bestowing their love upon him in earliest infancy.

One of the chief reasons for which people turn to third parties is their natural anxiety to have a baby as soon as possible after he is born, and as quickly as possible after they have made their important decision to adopt. Another advantage of the third-party arrangement is that the baby is spared the impersonal care of an institution. The new mother usually fetches the infant from hospital, or from a foster-mother who has cared for the infant for his first weeks of life.

A woman who had experienced both third-party arrangement and the methods of a voluntary adoption society told me: 'The third-party adoption seemed more natural, gentler, kinder . . . I collected one baby from a nursery where the atmosphere was altogether wrong . . . reminded me of battery farming . . . the other baby from a foster-mother who seemed a sweet person and who obviously adored him.' To this adopter the second baby had had a much better start and she had felt better about it too.

Another woman who had adopted two babies through a Harley Street doctor expressed similar contentment:[10] 'After tramping round the societies being asked every sort of interfering question about our lives, this was blissful, like having babies should be.' Religion, age, income, job, health, married or single state,[11] are immaterial in most third-party adoptions. References are rarely taken up and motives are not mistrusted, even if the adopters are taking a coloured or handicapped child.

Often a third-party adoption is a last resort of would-be adopters. Mr. H. W. Pring of the Surrey County Council, who has more than forty-five years of experience of welfare work among children, claims[12] he has never heard of any would-be adopters rejected by a third-party. 'Only too often one hears of people rejected not by one but by a number of societies, finding a child through one of these doubtful agencies.'

It also appears that many adopters, and in particular professional people, turn to third parties because they dislike being asked personal questions, often by social workers whom they may feel secretly are of lesser intelligence. Most of all they resent being asked for evidence of infertility, or sub-fertility, and clearly do not wish the responsibility for their childlessness to be apportioned. Rightly, they maintain this is their private concern, while the caseworker contends such couples are unlikely to make good adopters if they shirk facts about their own infertility and sexuality.

Many adoption workers believe that boys are less in demand to adopt because they are more of a sex symbol and so a torment to the sterile man, and that adoptive mothers are often made overanxious by their daughter's growing sexuality in adolescence and unable to tolerate the ordinary jealousies and conflicts that exist then because of their own inability to have children.

I was shown a caseworker's annual report by one registered society which included reasons for rejection of applicants. Obviously, the reasons were not fully explored, but superficially several seemed odd and arbitrary grounds for refusal. One applicant was written off as 'an unimaginative and potentially selfish father'. Another couple's claim was deferred until the husband lost weight. Two common reasons for rejection were 'too old', and 'having own family, or able to have own family'.

What is 'too old' to give a homeless child a loving home? Why should the experience of raising your own family preclude you from consideration as adopters? And are not many fathers unimaginative and selfish yet much loved and trusted by their families?

There is plenty of new thinking among workers in the registered agencies, but too many of the current fashions in adoption work appear to lack both commonsense and imagination. Worst, there is a tendency for some of the societies to become too bossy ('directive' is the polite sociological word) about the way to bring up children, and reluctant to let go of the adopters even when the child is legally theirs.

The Guild of Service, Edinburgh, invites adoptive parents to attend group meetings to discuss the special problems of bringing up adopted children. The groups are for parents of children aged $3\frac{1}{2}$ to $4\frac{1}{2}$ and for parents whose children are 5 to $6\frac{1}{2}$ years old. The Guild started the scheme experimentally but it became clear that the adopters found sharing their experience helpful and in some cases reassuring. All of them want to continue to keep in touch. Other societies, particularly Moral Welfare and Family Welfare Associations, organize meetings of adopters to hear a talk, express their views, and discuss their difficulties.

The idea appals me. When are adults going to be allowed to behave as adult? The 'group' is in vogue, but further corrodes the once valued strengths of self-reliance and independence. We do not need always to be leaning on one another and if adopters should meet serious difficulties, it is better for them to seek specialist advice in private. Adoption is essentially an intimacy for the family, not for harangue by the group. If the likelihood of difficulties is given too much emphasis, then difficulties will be met and group meetings may create an unwarrantable emphasis upon the innate differences of adopted families. These differences have already been accepted by good adopters.

Another fashionable idea in adoption is to arrange for the natural mother, and sometimes the father, to meet the prospective adopters. Two societies nearly always arrange a brief meeting between mother and adoptive parents at the time of placing the child and several others do this occasionally.[13] On the face of it this may sound a warm and human idea. It would save the mother giving her baby to faceless strangers and the adopters would be able to help their child with a first-hand description of his natural mother when he wanted details of his parentage. On the other hand, the mother is given details about the couple taking her baby by the adoption society, and she would be hard-pressed to find out as much about them for herself during a brief meeting in a contrived and tense situation. She might take an immediate dislike to the other woman but first impressions often mislead. In the same way the adopters have already been given much information about the baby's parents and background. To provide such an opportunity for instant and highly emotional judgements is to make a mockery of the casework supporting the adoption. At any rate, there is an urgent need for a close study of the benefits and problems which result from these meetings. Such intensely emotional confrontations have powerful long-term effects for good or ill.

Other revolutionary, and in my view, foolish proposals have been made to allow some continued contact between adopted children and their natural parents. One suggestion[14] has been that the adoption societies should act as a post office for correspondence between the concerned natural parent and the adopted child. There is a vital difference between laying a ghost (by giving the child the facts about his natural parents) and resurrecting it in this way. To my mind such an arrangement would create acute difficulties for the adoptive parents, particularly during adolescence when at some time every child is afflicted with 'double vision' and builds fantasies about superior parents.

What is called the 'genealogical bewilderment' of the adopted child is another new alarm.[15] Like the swan in Hans Andersen's *The Ugly Duckling* he is not understood; he does not 'belong'; he cannot identify with others differing from himself so much in appearance and performance. All this intellectual theorizing intimidates many prospective adopters. They become frightened by the cleverness of registered societies whose caseworkers seem intent on complicating the issue, and turn to third parties who keep it simple.

Too simple, many protest. Third parties are chiefly anxious to relieve the unmarried mother, or to help the childless couple, but the baby's interests are not of paramount importance. The obvious flaw in this complaint is that the baby's best interest in one most important respect is well served by being placed at birth or soon afterwards. Nor can it be seriously argued that he is in jeopardy of being adopted by flagrantly unsuitable people. The local authority investigates the home before the baby is received, and although this may be a perfunctory examination, there is the additional protection of the guardian *ad litem*'s inquiries. The guardian has to obtain a medical certificate from the prospective adopters. A report about the baby's health also goes before the court. A record of the natural mother's health should also be obtained. If the home and the adopters appear grossly unsatisfactory then the Adoption Order will be refused. If the child's well-being is threatened he will be removed.

The Hurst Committee[16] was reluctant to restrict third-party adoptions but they recommended that all third parties be made respondents to the application. This would mean that they would be served with notice of the application, be interviewed by the guardian *ad litem* and might also be required to attend the hearing, but the Hurst Committee's proposal has yet to be enforced.

There has also been the proposal[17] that all adopters should first be required to get a licence to adopt through the local authority, who would inquire into their credentials and capacities. If the applicants were refused a licence they would have the right of appeal to a court of law against the refusal. Only after a licence was granted could prospective adopters take a child into their care either through a registered agency or a third party.

The agencies would not object to this additional safeguard and third parties would be prevented from placing children with unsatisfactory or unsuitable people. After the child had been placed, if all went well, the licence would be endorsed after an interval and then the adoption would be registered in the same way as a marriage, either in a register office or at a church.

With licensing might also come a curtailment of the activities of the busy third parties. It could be made illegal for an individual to arrange more than one or two adoptions in a year. At present, knowledge of active third parties is dispersed. They must notify the local authority for the area in which the child is to be placed; but, if they also had to tell the local authority for the area in which they live, a clear picture of their activities would emerge.

Within the child-care profession there is a prejudiced dislike of the third-party arrangement, but there is no decisive research evidence in favour of adoption society practices.

Researchers in Connecticut in 1951[18] found one hundred agency placements more successful than one hundred private ones, but give meagre details about their methods of investigation. Another American researcher[19] found in 1967 that independently placed children are slightly superior on some tests, possibly because as babies they were healthier and more quickly adopted. In yet another American follow-up study[20] in 1963 of 484 children privately adopted between 1944–9, two-thirds were regarded as 'reasonably satisfactory' and another 10 per cent could not be classified as definitely unsatisfactory, while 85 per cent of the adoptive parents expressed unqualified satisfaction. A British investigator in 1958[21] found that the method of adoption had had no influence on the outcome.

These findings are too tenuous to build on. The American studies will be biased by the fact that in the United States the less acceptable infants are more often given to agencies to place and this factor may cancel out the advantage of a careful choice of home. More important, the time between the adoptions and the publication of these studies makes it unwise to claim that the findings are relevant to present-day practices. Some of the more bizarre placements would probably not occur today.

Some adoption agencies claim, almost with pride, that they place only a small number of babies because of the care and skill they lavish upon each adoption. Is this really justifiable when the needs of so many are so great? The alternatives to early adoption are so often crippling to the child's total development, and full of heartache for so many loving would-be adopters.

NOTES

1. Ellison, Mary, *The Deprived Child and Adoption* (Pan Books Ltd., 1963).
2. *Child Adoption No. 47* (Summer, 1965).
3. Letter to author, 18 June 1967, from Miss Jane Rowe, tutor and advisor to the S.C.S.R.A.
4. *Child Adoption No. 47* (Summer, 1965). Pring on 'Adoption'.
5. In the first instance to the local children's court.
6. The Hurst Committee Report of the Departmental Committee on the Adoption of Children. Cmnd. 9248 (H.M.S.O., 1954).
7. The Hurst Committee Report of the Departmental Committee on the Adoption of Children. Cmnd. 9248 (H.M.S.O., 1954).

8. Miss D. G. Hillier, for twenty-six years head of the adoption department of the Church of England Children's Society, commented on this fact in a series of articles on adoption in *The People*, December 1963.

9. Bayley, N. 'Mental Growth during the first three years', Worcester, Mass., 1933. Michaels, R. & Brenner, R. F.: A follow-up study of adoptive homes, New York (Child Adoption Committee of the Free Synagogue).

10. *The Sunday Times Weekly Review*, 17 July 1966.

11. There is nothing in adoption law debarring a single woman from adopting a child. A single man can adopt a boy but is not allowed to adopt a girl unless the court is satisfied there are exceptional circumstances.

12. *Child Adoption No. 47* (Summer, 1965). Pring on 'Adoption'.

13. *Child Adoption No. 51*, 1967: Jane Rowe, 'Present Standards and Future Needs'.

14. A letter from an adopted man in *Child Adoption*, No. 49, 1966.

15. Sants, H. J., 'Genealogical Bewilderment in Children with Substitute Parents'. (*Brit. J. Med. Psychol.*, 1964).

16. The Hurst Committee Report of the Departmental Committee on the Adoption of Children, Cmnd. 9248 (H.M.S.O. 1954).

17. *Child Adoption No. 47* (Summer, 1965). Pring on 'Adoption'.

18. Amatruda, C. S. and Baldwin, J. V., 'Current Adoption Practices' (*Journal of Paediatrics 38*, 208–12, 1951).

19. Wittenborn, J. R., *The Placement of Adoptive Children*, Springfield, Illinois, U.S.A. (1957).

20. Witmer, H. L. *Independent Adoptions*—a follow-up study, Russell Sage Foundation, New York (1963).

6

Institution Children

A MOTHER'S delight in feeding and bathing her newborn child is like the sun coming out for the baby.[1] He takes for granted his clothes will be soft, the bath water at the right temperature and his food suitable. But the mother's enjoyment has to be there or else the whole procedure is dead, useless, and mechanical. It is her pleasure in him which is his spiritual and emotional nourishment.

Experts, who so rarely agree, are unanimous in their strong opposition to institutions bringing up children for the simple reason that every baby needs mothering. The younger the child the more an institutional environment with its emphasis on bodily needs is to be deplored.

The most delicate part of a baby is his budding personality and no residential nursery can provide satisfactorily for the needs of infants. This is not just the belief of a few specialists obsessed with theoretical aspects of the problem; it is also the considered opinion of practical workers in many countries.

Running a wartime nursery, Mrs. D. Burlingham and Miss A. Freud[2] became increasingly aware of the difficulties of providing substitute care in an institutional setting. In the end they arranged for each helper to take a couple of children home and closed the nursery.

As long ago as 1938 a League of Nations Report drew attention to difficulties institutions experienced in caring for 'infants and very young children who appear to thrive better and to develop more quickly and vigorously under individual attention and in an atmosphere of family affection'.

Yet the myth persists that institutional conditions are harmless for babies and toddlers. In 1946 the Curtis Committee,[3] reporting

96

to the Government on the care of deprived children, actually recommended residential nurseries 'specially arranged to meet the needs of babies and giving highly skilled specialized attention to their physical health'. Such places are often havens of hygiene and administrative tidiness. The babies' systematic feeds are prepared in a Home Office regulated 'Milk-Room'. The nurseries are light, spacious, and polished. The nurses are young, cheerful, and detached. They wear trim uniforms and keep strict hours of duty. The children are their paid job, their means of training. It is all wonderfully clinical but far removed from a baby's real needs, a mother who loves and cares for him with constancy and enjoyment.

The immense contribution to the individual and to society which the ordinary good mother makes simply through being devoted to her infant, goes largely unrecognized. It is, nevertheless, immeasurable and extraordinarily difficult to provide for outside the family.

In New York City a large institution appeals for motherly women to go in and bestow upon the children what is known as 't.l.c.', tender love and care. It was the same thought which moved Bernard Shaw to write to *The Times* (21 July, 1944) suggesting that the trained nurse with no time to spare for cuddling the babies must be supplemented by 'affectionate masseuses'. He asked, 'Have we not enough motherly and grandmotherly women . . . to volunteer for this service, before and after they have reared their own children?'

Unfortunately many institutions still dislike too personal an interest to be taken in the babies by outsiders and, occasionally, even show resentment of the child's own relatives. Matrons can easily become possessive about 'their' children. Nevertheless, institutional children need the outside world and interruptions of their sterile routine. And, I suggest, the most promising source of 'maternal masseuses' could be honorary grannies, found among warm-hearted women in the Women's Institutes and kindred organizations. Honorary grandpas too would be a healthy corrective to the female domination of the nursery.

In his letter to *The Times*, Bernard Shaw contrasted life in a once world-famous institution for infants with conditions of

G

extreme poverty in Ireland. The Kaiserin Augusta's House in Berlin reared children with scientific efficiency, trained nurses, worked under the best medical advice, and the infants died like flies. Among the families living in mud cabins in Connemara there was no infant mortality rate. The Connemara mothers knew 'rather less about the scientific nurture of children than about electronic physics', but 'they hugged their babies, mammocked them, kissed them, smacked them, talked baby talk to them or scolded them: in short, maternally massaged them to their heart's content'.

There is a wealth of literature and continuing research into the effects of an absence of mothering. Dr. John Bowlby's report upon maternal care and mental health[4] concludes that to deny the young child a mother over a long period might have grave and far-reaching effects on his character and consequently on the whole of his future life. In fact, he says, the proper care of children without a normal home life is not merely an act of common humanity but essential to the mental and social welfare of a community.

Dr. Bowlby advocates determined action to reduce the number of deprived children in our midst. He deplores the sparsity of social workers trained to recognize psychiatric factors and able to deal with them effectively. Most importantly, he attacks the lack of conviction on the part of governments, social agencies, and the public, that mother-love is as important for mental health as are vitamins and proteins for physical health. 'Members of committees, in contemplating the fruits of their labours, are apt to find more personal satisfaction in visiting an institution and reviewing a docile group of physically well-cared for children than in trying to imagine the same children, rather more grubby perhaps, happily playing in their own or foster-homes.'

The impossibility of providing a permanent mother-substitute for each baby is not the only objection to a nursery. Institutional life is artificial. The child is denied family life and all that it teaches. The toddler in the 'Home' is not often short of toys, but he is bereft of the opportunity to take an active part in the rich routines of everyday life alongside a much loved adult. It is exceptional to find a two-year-old in an institution kneeling up at the kitchen sink with a washing-up mop, or rolling out putty-coloured pastry tarts. The number of children being cared for does not allow such fulfilling activities.

Because the baby does not learn the meaning of love in his mother's[5] arms he often grows up unable to give or receive affection. This is the worst and most destructive effect of an institutionalized infancy. There is danger that the child grows up emotionally undeveloped and unable to make enduring personal relationships. He tends to develop a superficial sociability and to become sexually promiscuous through pathetic attempts to assure himself of his own personal worth, his own lovability.

The development of the infant in an institution is slower than the normal from an early age, and the longer the deprivation continues the lower falls the child's rate of development. The deprived baby is unnaturally quiet. He may often fail to respond, fail to gain weight as he should in spite of good food, sleep badly, and show no initiative. A study[6] of infants' babbling and crying showed that babies from birth to six months in institutions were always less vocal than those in families, the difference being clearly noticed before two months. This backwardness in 'talking' is typical of the institutional child of all ages.

An older baby on being separated from his mother may cry painfully and continuously. This gives way to a period of mourning, the baby becoming withdrawn and sad. Then he appears 'to settle down'. This is, of course, wishful thinking on the part of those looking after him. In fact, he has just given up and, engulfed in feelings of hopelessness, becomes a detached easy-to-manage baby to whom one adult is as good as another. Studies in many countries are in impressive agreement upon the damaging effects of institutions upon the development of babies. Only a few of these investigations need be mentioned here.

In Denmark more than a hundred children,[7] aged one to four years, almost all of whom had spent their whole lives in one of twelve different institutions were compared with children who lived at home and attended day nurseries. The mothers of these children were working and the homes often unsatisfactory. Even so, the average 'development quotient'[8] of the children at home was normal while that of the institutional children retarded, and this difference is found consistently with children in their second, third, and fourth years of life.

A New York psychologist, Dr. W. Goldfarb,[9] compared the development of children brought up from soon after birth until about three in an institution and then placed in foster-homes, with other children who had gone directly from their mothers to foster-homes, in which they had remained. He took great care to make sure that fifteen pairs of children were of similar heredity. He examined them when they were aged ten to fourteen years. None of the children had a completely unbroken home-life, yet the difference between them was painfully full of meaning. In intelligence, power of abstract thinking, and social maturity, the institutional children fell far below the others.

Another American psychiatrist, Dr. L. G. Lowry,[10] found similar results after a study of children admitted to an institution before one and remaining until three or four, when they were transferred to another society for fostering. They were examined when they were five or older and all of them showed severe personality disturbances centring on an inability to give or receive affection. Their troubles included aggressiveness, contrariness, or obstinacy, selfishness, excessive crying, food difficulties, speech defects, bed-wetting and soiling, over-activity and fears. Both Dr. Goldfarb and Dr. Lowry suggest that every child who spends his early years in an institution will develop poorly.

Since these studies were carried out, most nurseries are managed in a more enlightened fashion; but the evidence of ill-effects among children who have spent long periods in them is much the same. A more recent study of children placed in British foster homes[11] shows an obvious connection between children removed from foster parents and earlier institutional care. More than three-quarters of children who 'failed' in their foster homes spent at least half the first three years of their lives in institutions. A poor capacity to give and receive affection accounted for 30 per cent of the broken foster arrangements. The failing is characteristically attributed to an institutional upbringing. This research discounts the suggestion sometimes made that a child separated from his parents needs an opportunity to recover from the experience in the undemanding atmosphere of a residential children's home before being placed in a private family. On the contrary, children from institutions more often 'failed' than others also being placed in a foster-home for the first time.

An American study in 1962[12] compared the development of seventy-five institution babies with an equal number of babies living at home during their first year of life. The institution babies were slow to acquire head control, to sit erect, to stand and to walk. From the eighth month onwards they showed less interest in toys and people, and reduced use of physical skills to explore their surroundings and to express their feelings. Backwardness in talking was evident early and became marked. Although an understanding of language was also retarded, it was talking that was most affected.

In their reactions to people the institution children were piteously different. They were slow to differentiate between people and neither developed a sense of trust nor sought help from an adult when in distress. Although an adequate number of toys was provided for the institution babies, they showed little interest in them, no displeasure at the loss of a toy and no effort to recover a lost toy. Spontaneous play by the babies was limited and altogether their range and intensity of feeling and expression greatly impoverished.

Christoph Heinicke[13] studied the behaviour of half a dozen children aged between one and three years during their first fortnight in a residential nursery; and he contrasted their behaviour with other children (matched for age and background) newly admitted at a day nursery. All the children protested against the separation, but the protests of those in the residential nursery were far greater. The day nursery children cried for only 2 or 3 per cent of the time, the residential children cried about five times as much, that is about five to seven minutes in every hour. For most of that time all the children were crying for mother. Children of both groups had opportunity to form attachments to nursery staff and did so, but those in the residential nursery formed more intense and ambivalent attachments, were more resistant to adult demands, and were given to more frequent episodes of hostility.

Children under three are deeply distressed and cry a great deal when they are away from home. Also, when they return home, even after only two or three weeks away in which they have been kindly treated, they have become increasingly anxious and apprehensive because they fear a repetition of the experience.

Currently, child experts are reviewing their theories in the light of ethology, and applying new knowledge of animal behaviour to some problems of childhood development. There is widespread interest in experiments which deprive animals of normal stimulation and such research is often drastic in conception and dramatic in result. The experiments have given rise to the suggestion that the key factor in maternal deprivation is inadequate stimulation from the environment and not the lack of relationship with a mother figure. The contention may be true of some animal species, but its application to children is extremely dubious. An unhappy child does not respond to his environment, however exciting and creative. It is 'only near his mother, or at least accessible to her, that a young child feels secure and has confidence to explore the world'.[14] Measures to enrich the institutional environment by providing nursery-school experience for children over two years are much less effective in stemming backwardness than are measures that give a child the chance to attach himself to a substitute mother.

Today the controversy about the effects of maternal deprivation is more a matter of qualification than contradiction. The research findings form a complicated but coherent body of evidence with no inherent conflict, only modifications.

A study of prediction in fostering in 1966[15] showed that the longer the child spent in institutional care the more adverse the effect on fostering. But it challenged the assumption that *any time* spent in an institution prejudices the chances of successful fostering. Children who had spent short periods in institutions before going to private families were found as likely to be successful, if not more so, than those children without institutional experience.

A number of studies show that many deprived children achieve a tolerable degree of social adaptation when adult. It would be a mistake, however, to build too much on this hope, because people who are psychologically disturbed often make an apparent adjustment for long periods.

Some investigations during the last decade attempt to assess more realistically the recovery powers of children who have been institutionalized, and to define the complex factors which determine the nature and severity of depriving experiences. It emerges clearly that the age of the child and the period of deprivation are important. Even now not enough is known to define precisely a critical phase, but some evidence suggests that during the second six months of life a baby is especially vulnerable to removal from mother.

The detailed findings of researchers into this area are too intricate and sophisticated to explore at length here.[16] Recent research, however, makes it quite clear that prolonged and severe deprivation from the early months of life if continued for three years usually causes permanent damage to both intellect and personality. Long-lasting deprivation which begins during the second year also leads to grave effects on personality, but general intelligence seems to be readily reawakened. The younger the infant when deprivation is relieved, the more normal is his later development.

Nothing encourages the optimistic view that the harm done to unmothered children can be completely repaired in time. Some effects of deprivation may be made good more readily, more completely and more frequently than was thought possible when Dr. Bowlby wrote his monograph in 1951. Nevertheless, there are limits to the improvements that can be expected when the damage is severe and of long standing.

The genetic endowment of the child affects his vulnerability, and possibly some children are too lightly regarded as recovered, when hidden and subtle effects persist and can be easily reactivated. The more superficial the assessment of damage, the more apparent evidence of recovery.

It is not accepted practice that children in nurseries should have psychological tests at regular intervals. In 1959 Dr. Bowlby advocated: 'If such tests were in use at least there would be knowledge of any psychological damage which was being done instead of, as at present, those responsible remaining in ignorance of the matter and able blandly to affirm that the children are perfectly all right.'

Some enlightened local authorities and voluntary societies have closed residential nurseries (or curtailed their use) and found foster-mothers for babies awaiting adoption or restoration to their mothers. Other councils and charities have divided their nurseries into small 'family' units, each group having its own pair of rooms, for sleeping and for eating and playing.

It is sound policy, theoretically, for a nurse to be given a particular child, or children, to care for; but the inevitable regimen of an institution means that nurses, unlike most mothers of babies, go on and off duty. I believe it is attempting the impossible to provide mother-love in a nursery which also trains young staff.

Discipline, starch, and textbooks all get in the way; and matron is often hospital-trained. Many matrons are not easily persuaded to change their spotless uniforms for the working clothes busy mothers wear. Nurses like a uniform too. Perhaps because it proclaims that they are not pushing out their own babies but other people's. Management committees also look upon the nursing uniforms as a good advertisement for 'the Home', revealing a quaint pride in a form of charity as outmoded as the old workhouse and possibly even more disastrous in its effects.

Fortunately, today, large institutions for older children are officially deplored although they have not yet disappeared. One old-fashioned and forbidding institution, the Aberlour Orphanage in the north of Scotland, was shown on television[17] only three years ago. This 'Home' to 160 children had its own church and school and there was little or no opportunity for mixing with local children. Aberlour, founded by Church and charity a hundred years ago, costs £70,000 a year to run. In the television programme the children were seen to follow a regimented life inevitable in an institution of such size. But plans were already prepared for modernizing. Today the Aberlour Trust has closed this old-style orphanage and opened ten homes housing from six to twenty children who now attend local schools and churches.

The 'cottage-home' is now the accepted provision, but the name conjures up a cosily false picture. Cottage homes may house up to twenty children, and so many are often placed together that they create a false community of several hundreds of deprived children. Grouping cottage-homes gives more support to the house-parents and saves money on some common services at the expense of the children. They are denied the opportunity of being readily absorbed into the life of a neighbourhood. For example, Essex had 250 children in a cottage-homes community in 1965.

This loss of initiative and removal of responsibility is unhealthy, and to overcome it the 'scattered' cottage-home is recommended. The arrangement is still artificial and can be described as a large professional foster-home. Many local authorities buy semi-detached houses in suburbs or on new housing estates where a married couple will take care of six to twelve children. The man goes out to work, the wife 'mothers' and the children mix with the local children.

Even in relatively favourable circumstances like these it remains difficult to avoid some of the undesirable characteristics of the institution. Six children is a large family by normal standards. Six deprived children (and this is an unusually small number) are a much more demanding family. The house-mother is rare, probably non-existent, who can feel or effect strong and equal affection for all the many children entrusted to her. What is really calamitous is the high turnover of staff in residential children's homes (about 35 per cent change jobs annually),[18] children's frequent changes of placement (on average once every two years)[19] and the continual coming and going of other children.

It is trite to say that men and women genuinely devoted to children and gifted in looking after them are needed as house-mothers and fathers; but it is difficult to imagine the arduous and often heart-rending tasks they assume. The children need intensive mothering; but among other things, a house-parent must not attempt to own the children and should encourage parents to visit. In 1951 John Bowlby wrote: 'That house-mothers require training and that their work should be put on a professional basis is now recognized.'[20] Unfortunately this professionalism certainly is not evident today. Quite untrained people are often accepted because there is nobody else.

An inquiry[21] into the problems of staffing local authority residential homes for children found that the most common dissatisfactions were excessive hours of work, the difficulty of taking time off, the poor standard of accommodation provided (particularly insufficient privacy), and problems in staff relationships. Obviously child care in residential homes has become an increasingly unattractive career for women.

Older children seem to adapt more easily to institutional life. They develop a double standard of morals: an external obedience to regulations; and an internal standard which may be thoroughly delinquent and which only declares itself later. Their behaviour is deceptive. Outwardly they appear cheerful and conforming; inwardly, there is turbulence, anger, and often impenetrable grief.

Children after a long time in an institution often seem 'nice and polite' but when found foster-homes they are frequently afraid of close personal contacts and seem to prefer living in an emotional vacuum. They avoid decisions, resent suggestions of independence and make excessive demands for pocket-money, clothes, and 'treats'. These traits only emerge when they leave the institution: while they were in it all seemed well, to the untrained eye at any rate.

An examination[22] of a group of children aged six to eight, none of whom was considered in any way abnormal by those who ran the institution in which they lived, produced surprises. They were summed up as 'affectionless and sick characters, masquerading as normal children'. As might be expected, they had been brought up in the institution from an early age.

It is when they leave the undemanding environment of the institution that children are liable to go to pieces. A young man of twenty-one who appeared on the ITV programme on children in care,[23] made the point: 'Suddenly you've got a hundred and one things to do for yourself which you didn't have when you was under authority . . .' He had had ten jobs in six years. 'Sometimes I got the sack, sometimes I couldn't get up early in the mornings to get there, or I was late, something like that. I've left jobs, good jobs in fact I've left, mainly because I've moved away, you see, restlessness.'

The best-run institution is too removed from ordinary life. Moreover, many residential homes, especially nurseries, still lack a father-figure, which makes identification with a man difficult. Young children tend to fasten themselves on to any man who might visit the home and call him 'Daddy'. Later this deprivation of a father-figure curtails their opportunities to learn about happy and loving relationships between adult men and women.

How does a child who has never known good parents become one himself? Too often the pattern drearily repeats itself, deprived children become in turn depriving parents.

It is more than time that these institutions were closed. They are a boon to administrators but adoption societies and local authorities should arrange adoptions, not run Homes.

Many people feel there is something sacrosanct about parents' rights. But parents who appear neither able nor willing to bring up their children should no longer have rights in their offspring. If they cannot or will not act as parents, someone else should be allowed to, and quickly. If not the children pay the penalty of neglect, an appalling price of part-lived promise and the pains of a childhood without love.

Such a major reform would do away with much of the need for long-term fostering, which is but an uncertain compromise between the strength and love that an adoptive home should give, and the emotional sterility of the institution. Children in institutions are patronized with treats, teas, toys, and discarded clothing. A child's drawing I saw pinned up in the Matron's office at one Home was a picture in red crayon. Underneath was written in careful script: 'Tea in the Kind Lady's House'. The effort and money which goes into running and staffing these institutions should be diverted now into the urgent job of finding parents for all homeless children, not forgetting the coloured and the handicapped.

NOTES

1. Winnicott, D. W., *The Child, the Family, and the Outside World* (Penguin Books, 1964).

2. Burlingham, D. and Freud, A., 'Monthly Report of Hampstead Nurseries' for May 1944 (unpublished). 'Young Children in War-time', London (1942). 'Infants without Families', London (1943).

3. Report of the Care of Children Committee (The Curtis Committee) (H.M.S.O., 1946).

4. Bowlby, J., 'Maternal Care and Mental Health,' *World Health Organization Monograph* Series No. 2, 1951. Bowlby's views are little changed. A 1965 paperback edition, *Child Care and the Growth of Love*, offers identical conclusions.

5. Mother or permanent mother-substitute, one person who steadily mothers the child.

6. Brodbeck, A. J. & Irwin, O. C. *Child Development*, **17**, 145 (1946).

7. Simonsen, K. M., 'Examination of children from children's homes and day nurseries', Copenhagen (1947).

8. The development quotient, although calculated in a way similar to the intelligence quotient (I.Q.) is concerned with general physical and mental development, of which intelligence is only a part. A D.Q. of 90 to 110 represents average development.

9. Goldfarb, W., *J. exp. Educ.* **12**, 106 (1943).

10. Lowry, Dr. L. G., *Amer. J. Orthopsychiat.* **10**, 576 (1940).

11. Trasler, Gordon, *In Place of Parents* (Routledge & Kegan Paul, 1960).

12. Provence, S. and Lipton, R. C., *Infants in Institutions* (International Universities Press, New York, 1962).

13. Heincke, C. M., 'Some effects of separating two-year-old children from their parents: a comparative study'. *Hum. Relat.* **9**, 105 (1956).

14. Bowlby, John, 'Security and Anxiety', *The Listener*, 17 March 1966.

15. Parker, R. A., *Decision in Child Care* (George Allen and Unwin Ltd., 1966.)

16. They are discussed fully by Dr. Mary D. Salter Ainsworth in the Penguin edition of Bowlby's work where he contributes two new chapters on these issues.

17. ITV 'This Week', *Children in Care*, 9 December 1965.

18. Pringle Kellmer, M. L., An essay on 'Positive Child Care and Education' in *Investment in Children* (Longmans, Green, 1965).

19. Ibid.

20. Bowlby, J., *Maternal Care and Mental Health*, World Health Organization, Monograph Series No. 2, (1951).

21. Social Survey, 1963.

22. Bettelheim, B. & Sylvester, E. *Amer. J. Orthopsychiat*, **18**, 191 (1948).

23. ITV 'This Week', *Children in Care*, 9 December 1965.

7

Handicapped Children

Many officials ruin a child's opportunities and sentence him to an unhappy and unfulfilled life by labelling him 'unsuitable for adoption'. The judgement is both iniquitous and tragic. If capable adopters know sufficient about the baby and are prepared to love him, they should be given help and encouragement. Far too often idealism is equated with eccentricity and high motives frustrated by the circumspection of caseworkers with their analytical wariness of the enthusiasm of love.

Offers were made to adopt thalidomide babies, whose families may have rejected them or felt unable to look after them. This indeed is evidence of a remarkable love and compassion; although the sophisticated reaction is probably one of doubt about the 'suitability' of such people to assume these demanding responsibilities.

It is abundantly obvious that young children need parents, and handicapped children need them most of all: to the desolation of a child bereft of parents is added the fearful loneliness of disablement, which too often estranges a man from his fellows. The great need of handicapped children is for love and acceptance, not segregation and special homes, however good the training and dedicated the staff. They need to belong to the world, not to be cut off from it.

The charitable, but cowardly, solution to the problem has long been the establishment of special schools and homes. But it is, in a sense, conscience-money which supports them. Of course, sympathy and concern are felt but mostly a deep relief that the children are to be looked after in residential institutions, away from us all. Much ignorance, fear, and superstition still surround

109

the abnormal and a primitive reservoir of resentment can be called upon to put on one side the deformed child who is also a bastard.

The institution is seized upon as the most efficient solution. The children are together in expert hands and their disabilities discreetly contained within substantial houses and large gardens. Their welfare becomes the object of a frenzy of charity: coffee mornings, sales of work, fêtes and socials all raise money for their benefit. They are cared for by many, loved by none.

A hundred years ago Dr. Barnardo opposed segregation for handicapped children. He believed they had a richness of their own and could give as well as receive. In his experience 'they evoked the loving care and unselfish, generous treatment of their fellows, while they themselves, when playing with those who had no physical handicap, almost forgot that they were crippled and shook off the shyness and timidity so often associated with bodily deformity'.[1] The disabled child is often uniquely qualified to release the energy of love in another human being. This moving illustration is reported by D. M. Dyson in her book on foster-care.[2]

John is the spastic son of a family who fostered Susan, and the little girl became devoted to the crippled boy. 'She found a happiness which she could only have found in giving, and the foster-family's gratitude for the happiness she gave John undoubtedly strengthened the bonds of affection between them and her. . . . It is not always the easiest situations which enable children to develop their most precious qualities.'

It is assumed that child care today is, in the main, enlightened and progressive. There is certainly much talk about the challenge of the homeless children who are difficult to place with adopters; it is admitted by one specialist journal[3] that 'precious little quantitatively is yet being done'. The writer continues, 'Any society which is the chief or only adoption agency in its area and has not both the will and the facilities to cope with children who are handicapped cannot be said to be doing its job properly.'

In fact, only half the voluntary adoption societies accept

children with more than minor handicaps of health or background and even fewer place many coloured children.

Both handicapped and coloured children will often be accepted into the care of local authorities or children's welfare organizations but are seldom offered for adoption.

The category 'unsuitable for adoption' is given fantastically wide interpretation. Broadly, it covers children who have mental or physical disabilities, or a poor family history, or older children, or those who are coloured or of mixed ancestry. In some societies a child may not be offered for adoption if one of its parents was sent to an approved school, or if he is his mother's second or third illegitimate child. A birth mark, hare lip, or cleft palate, are believed to make a child unadoptable, and such children may be automatically transferred for permanent care to a children's home. Children of incest, criminals, and prostitutes are regarded as poor 'risks' and fears of any association with venereal disease frequently exaggerated.

Jane Rowe of the Standing Conference of Societies Registered for Adoption, wrote recently: 'Adoptive parents are often bolder and more broad-minded than social workers give them credit for and people vary in their attitudes towards risk.'[4] Clearly, the fears of the adoption agencies are depriving many children of parents, many homes of children. Adoption is felt to be too great a 'risk' on account of the child's health or heredity—or the agency, sometimes without really trying to find one, cannot believe a suitable home can exist for the child.

Research studies and practical experience offer no grounds for many of the common misgivings about adoption of handicapped children. On the contrary, they give cause for optimism. The biggest threats to successful adoption lie in brain damage which cannot always be detected in infancy, and in emotional damage caused by institutional care.

Parents and adopters are prepared to stand by their children through a range of serious illnesses but many are unable to love and care for children with severe mental defects. A child specialist[5] has suggested that it should be possible to revoke an adoption order if brain damage shows itself later in childhood. The suggestion is a good one because it aims to find babies parents as quickly as possible rather than delaying arrangements for uncertain medical forecasts.

On the other hand, a revocable adoption seems unnecessary because adopters with an imbecilic child can relieve themselves of their charge in the same way as an ordinary family facing this problem: the mentally deficient child whose parents cannot manage him will be found a place in an institution. Only mad children or those incurably ill and beyond any help a home can offer should be in institutional care. But if the worst happens, and the child's condition seriously deteriorates or he becomes unmanageable at home, what has been lost? He has at least known a fragment of love.

Folly lies in keeping children without a completely clean bill of health in institutional care to see if their condition can be improved before seeking adopters. The baby may be suffering from a minor eye or ear infection; but, whatever his troubles, to delay adoption and keep him in care will certainly create other disadvantages. He will be older and so less acceptable, and he will probably appear backward, unresponsive, and emotionally sterile. The longer he spends 'in care', not only the less likely he will be to find adopters, but the lower the chances of a happy outcome.

The Guild of Service, Edinburgh, who believe fervently in the long-term value of high-pressure casework, are proud of the fact that decisions 'about the adoptability or otherwise of our children are not made by social workers alone, but only after consultation with the appropriate expert'. This is certainly commendable, although consulting an expert seems an obvious course to take, but the most eminent paediatrician is guilty of exceeding his authority in dubbing a child as 'unadoptable'.

The Hurst Report[6] criticized adoption agencies who were chary of placing handicapped children. Incredibly, they also found it necessary to castigate some courts who even refused to grant an adoption order when the child was not completely healthy. The Committee recommended a schedule of health matters on which information should be obtained, but was explicit that, 'No provision should be made for any doctor to express an opinion of the suitability of the child for adoption. . . . This is a matter for the applicants to decide when they know the facts.'

It is a popular and frightening myth that a child inherits his parents' bad traits. 'Bad blood' is the sinister expression commonly heard, usually referring to criminal or sexually shocking behaviour. No one has yet shown, however, that children separated in early life from criminal or anti-social parents repeat the same patterns of behaviour. Criminal behaviour is an acquired characteristic and runs in families not because of 'heredity' but environment and upbringing. Again, 'heredity' determines our sex, not our sex lives; this is conditioned by a lack of family security and affection.

Children resulting from incest are often barred from the opportunities of adoption, although the risk of abnormality arising from incest is considered to be no greater than from the union of first cousins which also slightly increases the abnormality rate. On this evidence outright rejection of these children as unadoptable is unjustifiable.

Only one adopter of a handicapped child expressed any regrets about it in Witmer's[7] study of independent adoptions in America. Moreover, an earlier piece of research by Evans[8] found that 75 per cent of the parents who adopted handicapped children applied to adopt more. Medical care was needed for 80 per cent of the children. The parents felt some anxiety about this and needed support from the caseworker, but it was not necessary to make extra visits for this purpose. It is interesting that the adopters of these disabled children had a higher than average record of physical handicaps themselves.

Handicapped children feature prominently in inter-country adoptions and the results are encouraging. In May 1960 experts from sixteen countries met at Leysin to consider the problems of inter-country adoption. Their report reached the heartening conclusion that a vast number of couples throughout the world are anxious to give a deprived child the love of parents in a good home, whatever his initial handicap.

It was observed with compassion and realism: 'Remarkable examples have been seen of courageous couples completely

H

accepting as their own a child whom they know can never be like other children. . . . There are couples who genuinely want children and who believe that children should not be sentenced to grow up in an institution because of known or unknown factors in their background. The results of this experience have been decidedly positive. To those who say it is too soon to tell, consideration should be given to what the alternative represents for many children. . . .'

International Social Service[9] frequently acts as an intermediary between the natural parents and adopters in different countries. The organization safeguards the interests of the child by its thorough inquiries and ensures that the adoption is legalized. Several years ago I.S.S. organized a number of adoptions of homeless Greek children in America. Many of the children were so far below the medical standards required for obtaining American visas that the Greek branch of I.S.S. placed them first with foster-parents in the hope that they would improve with individual care. Eventually, almost all the children were able to travel to America and settled with the families who had asked for them.

The supreme value of early placing and the therapy of good fostering is also borne out by the Jewish Child Care Association of New York. They succeeded in placing children whose morbid family history and backward or maladjusted behaviour at one time precluded them from adoption. These children were boarded out in babyhood with good foster parents. Many became stable and affectionate and a large number of foster mothers asked to adopt them and were allowed to do so.

Chinese babies have been successfully adopted in American and British homes. Relatives of American coloured servicemen who gave children to British women, have been able to adopt these children. There is growing realization that adoption should not be reserved only for those children who are as near to 'ideal' as possible. Nevertheless, some countries still hold narrow views and uninformed prejudices.

The Swedish Board of Health and the Child Welfare Board is biased against permitting childless Swedish couples to adopt refugee children of other races. These authorities claim that the refugees would not be 'assimilated' among the fair-haired, fair-skinned Swedish community. In Britain almost every local council and every voluntary society have a large proportion of coloured and mixed race children who are available for adoption if parents could be found. But there is little evidence of an energetic recruitment of homes for these children; on the contrary, most voluntary societies will not even put coloured children on the adoption list.

The common practice seems to be to wait until someone actually asks for a coloured child. The would-be adopters are investigated exhaustively: do they want the baby as a protest against apartheid; or do they regard a negroid baby as a new kind of fashion, a novel kind of status symbol? Their good intentions may well be displaced by resentment and anger at questioning which only half conceals these insulting suggestions.

The British Adoption Project was launched in 1965[10] to investigate the problems of adopting a non-European baby in Britain. This research project will last four years and during this time it is planned to place fifty to sixty coloured babies with adopters in London and the Home Counties. These parents will be partners in the research. It seems almost incredible to report that even allowing that the first six months of the project was devoted to administration, after a year only six babies had been placed. This after press publicity and the distribution of 12,000 leaflets to children's departments, libraries, public baths, W.I.s, health visitors, and moral welfare workers, and Church bodies.

Couples who responded to these appeals were invited to small group meetings. Then, if they were still interested, a series of interviews awaited them. There were office interviews separately and together; home interviews and personal visits to referees, parents and relatives. The then director of the project, Miss Mary King, said one of its aims was to define basic qualities needed in adoptive parents. Obviously, if they were ever to receive a coloured child, patience, tolerance, and a sense of humour about the caseworker's tactics must have come high on the list. A conclusion Miss King offered, with some excitement, was that the adopters of coloured children would need to care less about what other people thought. Does it really need this kind of project which, although it is planned over four years, stops short of the critical times in a coloured child's life, going to school and starting work, to underline the obvious?

There should be far less of this fashionably intensive casework and more practical help given to those who are prepared to love children with difficulties. For example, laundry services for enuretic children, on the same lines as those run by some welfare departments for incontinent old people, may well mean the difference between keeping or returning a child. It may sound a poor parent who cannot love a bed-wetter; but many disturbed or backward children are slow to gain control in toilet training and any impatience on the part of those faced with the washing is likely to make matters worse. More help in the home would also be welcomed because any handicapped child is even more demanding than a normal one. It is better and cheaper to relieve natural or substitute mothers of some chores rather than of their children.

Some adoption societies like applicants for a handicapped child to have teaching or nursing experience, although advisory and specialist services are plentifully provided today. What the experts cannot give is 'mothering' and there should be more strenuous attempts at finding homes for handicapped children. The Curtis Committee[11] found that advertising and publicity aimed at idealism brought results, and I cannot subscribe to the widespread feeling that it is wrong to arouse emotion and conscience about all these children.

NOTES

1. Williams, A. E., *Barnardo of Stepney* (George Allen & Unwin Ltd., 1943).

2. Dyson, D. M., *No Two Alike* (George Allen & Unwin Ltd., 1962).

3. *Child Adoption, No. 51*, 1967.

4. Rowe, Jane, *Parents, Children and Adoption* (Routledge & Kegan Paul, 1966).

5. Professor J. P. M. Tizard (Professor of Paediatrics, Institute of Child Health and Post-Graduate Medical School, London University) put forward this idea at a day conference in London on the Unmarried Mother and Her Child in relation to Adoption on 26 October 1966. The conference was organized by the Medical Group of Standing Conference of Societies Registered for Adoption.

6. Report of the Departmental Committee on the Adoption of Children, Cmnd. 9248 (H.M.S.O., 1954).

7. Witmer, H. L., 'Independent adoptions—a follow-up study', Russell Sage Foundation, New York (1963).

8. Evans, H. R., 'Placing the handicapped child for adoption', *Catholic Charities Review*, **36**, 33–7 (1953). Condensed report of thesis for Master of Social Work degree, University of Nebraska.

9. The International Social Service of Great Britain was founded after the First World War to help refugees, but it has become increasingly concerned with the problems of homeless children.

10. Joint sponsors are Bedford College, London University, and International Social Service, with the backing of the Home Office.

11. Report of the Care of Children Committee (The Curtis Report), Cmnd. 6922 (H.M.S.O., 1964).

8

Fostered Children

FOSTERING homeless children is a compromise solution, for it provides homes without parents. Modern foster-parents are usually discouraged from behaving like parents. They are told to act as caretakers, to welcome the natural parents, and to remain unpossessive about the children. More and more they are being employed as colleagues in a professional job, and the outcome is that fostering, like all compromises, has become a matter of convenience rather than of success.

At worst the system can lead to total failure and inflict new wounds on children already damaged. Often foster-homes fail them so rapidly that children need new 'parents' every year. As a result many children grow up contemptuous of the concepts surrounding the words 'mother' and 'father' and with their trust in the world eroded, if not destroyed. More seriously their self-esteem sinks lower with each fresh experience of rejection.

The tragedy of these failures is ironically heightened by the attractive prospects fostering appears to offer. It seems such a good idea. The Curtis Committee,[1] aware of the shortcomings of the system, described it as second-best to adoption, but preferable to keeping children in institutions. Their recommendation of the compromise gave a strong impetus to the recruitment of foster-parents, and three years later the Children's Act of 1948 explicitly instructed local authorities with children in care to board them out whenever possible. Certainly, foster-homes hold out hopes of a more normal background, a richer life than the best of institutions can provide, and an infinitely more realistic preparation for adulthood. But for too many children a foster-home is an empty promise: it does not last. Perhaps the most important

118

underlying reason for this is the lack of commitment inherent in the principle of fostering. True parents want to do more than simply provide a good home for their children. Often they feel they have no choice but to accept wider socially approved implications of their roles, even when these demand sacrifices of personal ambitions and the quality of their own lives in order to advance the prospects of their children. Such considerations do not apply to foster-parents, and society exerts no similar pressures upon them. Foster-parents are regarded as people kind-hearted enough to open their homes to a special kind of lodger, and, just as the unconventional or difficult adult lodger is not to be tolerated, so social sympathy is readily available for those who reject their child 'guests' as too much of a strain.

It is the 'on approval' aspect of the arrangement which makes fostering a rotten second-best to adoption. It does not matter to an adult if he is not accepted unreservedly, unconditionally into someone else's house or family life: he does not expect to be. A child needs a home, not merely accommodation, and has to be accepted in this way. In all too many cases, however, he cannot be sure even of the roof over his head, for foster-parents are free to ask for his removal; social workers may elect to take him away; and his own parents, even if strangers to him, may claim him at any time. He may be unaware of any of these eventualities, but the insecurity of his position will almost inevitably be communicated to him. Insecurity is part of the climate of compromise which surrounds him.

The compromise seems to work tolerably well until a crisis erupts. A photograph showing anguish on the face of a child in West Berlin appeared in the Dutch magazine *Margriet* on 29 January 1966. An article explained that the child, aged six, was placed with foster-parents at eighteen months, after his mother had disappeared while he was in hospital. The foster-parents had never told him that he was not their natural son—he was not a strong child and they were anxious to shield him—and now more than four years later the natural mother was reclaiming the boy. Neighbours who watched the incident thought a child was being kidnapped. He was; the 'kidnapping' was legal. In similar circumstances, a mother might legally demand the return of her child from foster-parents in this country, and an investigation by the *Daily Mail* in 1967 revealed that such cases are by no means exceptional in Britain. The newspaper told of a girl placed with foster-parents soon after birth, whose natural mother wanted her back when she was six. Although mother and child had rarely met, the little girl was taken from the only home she knew and placed in the unfamiliar world of the mother. A *Daily Mail* editorial[2] reported that after publication of this story enough letters were received to suggest that similar cases were commonplace.

Many British newspapers in July 1967 reported that a girl was taken from foster-parents in Worcestershire by her mother whom she had not seen for twelve years. It takes little imagination to appreciate the appalling distress caused to foster-children and their foster-parents in these cases, and it is important to consider what might be done to ensure that such traumatic upheavals cannot occur. The new legislation required would cut right across deeply entrenched ideas of 'blood ties' and parental 'rights', but it would give statutory expression to the child's right to expect a real home, and to the principle that with parenthood goes the responsibility to meet this fundamental need.

The effective way to give children in foster-homes the security essential to a fruitful childhood is to remove from negligent natural parents control over their children's lives. Those who will not provide for their child within a reasonable period of time should lose parental rights and these should automatically be invested in the agency caring for the child. Parents could appeal to a court of law for an extension of the statutory time allowed to them to make a home for the child. The onus would be upon them to prove and declare their interest.

This is a drastic solution[3] which would arouse deep opposition and many so-called 'moral objections'. I will review the most obvious of these later. It is sufficient to say here that in my view the sexual act which leads to new life is the beginning of new responsibilities, which must be either totally accepted by one or both of the parties or totally delegated. Sanctimonious and hypercritical twaddle results from long debate about safeguarding parental rights when neither parent cares enough to embrace and cherish the new life they have created but will not let the child go.

Such a child is nobody's child. He may be visited spasmodically by a mother who has fast become a stranger, or he may wait in vain. Some day, she promises, she will take him home; but that day never comes. He passes his childhood in an institution or foster-home, or more likely, a series of foster-homes.

I suggest that parents should be compelled to reach a firm decision about their child's future within a year of placing him in care. An extension of time, up to a maximum of another six months, might be available on appeal, and even this would probably be erring on the generous side in view of all the evidence of damage from prolonged maternal deprivation. Research findings are complicated by qualifications but it is certain that the younger the infant when deprivation is relieved, the more normal will be his later development. Institutional life produces ill-effects in the early months and, if continued for three years, usually causes permanent damage to the child's intelligence and personality. One of the most distressing effects of an institutionalized infancy is that the unmothered baby grows up unable to be constant in friendship or love. The most sensitive phase in the young child's development has not been pinpointed, but some evidence indicates that a baby is particularly vulnerable to removal from his mother, or foster-mother, between six months and a year.

Even if the child is not institutionalized but receives plenty of mothering in a good foster-home, the experience must be brief or he will suffer when separated from his foster-mother, so quickly and strongly does a baby attach himself. One investigator[4] observed that only a few babies of three months showed any upset behaviour after removal from foster-homes compared with 86 per cent of six-months old babies. And all the babies who changed 'mothers' after seven months showed severe disturbance.

Nothing causes more damage than the willingness of local councils and agencies to accept children from parents on a temporary basis without any plans for the future. Instead of abetting irresponsibility, agencies, both statutory and voluntary, must make it their first consideration to help the parent, or parents, to formulate a practical plan for the future, and to make it clear that their help depends on a long-term solution being found within a reasonable time. After all, the alternatives are few and simple: the parents can themselves provide for the care of the child or release him for permanent placement.

Parents, even 'bad' parents, must never be patronized by social workers. Often the world's misery is less damaging than the world's charity. Good, bad, or indifferent parents are vital people in the lives of their children, and they should be persuaded to realize this and to share in the planning of the child's future. If they are left out of the picture, they are merely likely to interfere in haphazard and destructive ways which will ruin any chance of successfully fostering the child.

The success or failure of fostering as a system is a question at the heart of any consideration concerning deprived children. It is as central an issue as third-party adoptions, and yet, once again a matter not publicly ventilated by official bodies. The fact that the number of children 'in care' boarded out by local authorities increases by leaps and bounds—from less than 35 per cent twenty years ago to 50 per cent in 1966–7—cannot by itself be accepted as an endorsement of success. In fact, recent research studies in this country suggest that between a third and a half of foster-homes found by local authorities fail. The criterion for failure in these studies is the child's removal from the home, and there was no attempt to discriminate between some of the subtler forms of failures and success.

Research by Gordon Trasler[5] in the late nineteen-fifties suggested that between one-third and two-fifths of all long-term placements fail. R. A. Parker's[6] inquiry six years later showed nearly half the foster-homes failed.

A piece of work still being analysed in 1967 was an examination of the lives of children committed by juvenile courts to the care of three different local authorities. Arthur Collis, senior lecturer in Social Study at the University of Birmingham and responsible for the project, discovered that in 1945 these children were being moved on average once every two years; by 1950 once every fifteen months, and in 1955 once a year. If the child returned to the same home this was not counted as a 'move'. One boy was moved no fewer than seventeen times.

In both Parker's and Trasler's researches more than 70 per cent of the failures occurred within two years, and their work confirmed that the younger the child the better the chance of success. Parker found children under three the most successful in foster-homes, and those less than a year old had about a three to one chance of the arrangement being a success. Children of eleven and over faced a three to one chance of failure. Trasler reached similar conclusions: 69 per cent of the children under four were successfully placed, but the proportion dropped to only 40 per cent among children of four years and more.

These researchers are in broad agreement about the ill-effects upon fostering of a prolonged period in institutions. More than three-quarters of the children Trasler found to have failed in foster-homes had been taken into care before five and had spent at least half of their first three years in institutions. Parker's study also concluded that the longer the institutionalization the worse the effect on fostering. The highest rate of failure (74 per cent) was found among those children who had spent three years or more in institutions. Parker's research also suggests that children who spend only short periods in institutions are likely to be as successful, if not more so, than those who had had no institutional experience. He found, too, that those children who had been fostered once already were more successful with the second placing, maybe because successful adjustment in a foster-home can be learnt from experience. Placing a foster-child with a family, where there is already a child of the same sex and around the same age, is likely to cause friction and situations of jealousy and rivalry.

It is commonly found that older women make the most successful foster-parents although they frequently take older children who are the more difficult. Possibly this is because, having brought up their own children, they are more relaxed and confident in their handling of the foster-child. Foster-mothers under forty often fail because they are hoping the fostered child will become a companion for their own.

Trasler found an important reason for failure was when childless couples regarded the foster-child as a substitute for their own. On the other hand, Miss D. M. Dyson's conclusion[7] that childless couples often make excellent foster-parents is confirmed by Parker's study which showed 67 per cent childless foster-parents to succeed compared with 46 per cent of couples with children. Also, contrary to popular belief successful fostering does not necessarily depend on a married couple. Trasler's research suggests that foster-homes without a father are slightly more successful than those with both partners. The number of fatherless foster-homes in Parker's study was small but he too found these were no less successful than the others: of twelve foster-homes where there was only a foster-mother, nine succeeded.

Parker demonstrated a relationship between a child's bereavement and his failure in a foster-home. Of those children whose mothers were dead, 76 per cent failed compared with 44 per cent of children whose mothers were alive. Many factors are clearly related to each other: for example, the death of the child's mother is prejudicial, but bereaved children are also older at fostering and this too is an unfavourable factor. Parker eventually produced a table of factors which might be used to forecast failure in the foster-homes, scoring each situation as a guide to its importance:

1. There is a child of the foster-parents under five (33).
2. The child's own mother is dead (28).
3. The child is four or more (23).
4. The child has shown behaviour problems (17).
5. The child has not been previously fostered (15).
6. There is a child of the foster-parents whose age is within five years of that of the foster-child (14).

When this table was applied to the original sample it showed that a score of less than fifteen (none of the six adverse factors present) indicated a 94 per cent chance of success, and a score of eighty or more a mere 16 per cent prospect. The table was applied to one or two other samples and as a rule-of-thumb method of prediction found reasonable confirmation.

In view of the common occurrence among deprived children of at least one or more of the factors which make up Dr. Parker's gloomy table, it is not surprising perhaps that less than 20 per cent of the children in the care of the voluntary organizations are boarded out. More importantly, some societies are unconvinced that foster-homes are valuable and others impose rigid religious requirements which make it difficult to find suitable foster-parents. Almost all the voluntary societies are short of staff to find and supervise foster-homes, and, anyway, have many residential homes for children. The recommendations of the Children's Act 1948 were explicit that local authorities were to board out children with private families whenever possible, but the voluntary bodies received no such directive. When they do board out, the charities pride themselves on taking more care over placings than most local authorities. Certainly their failure rate is low, but it must be remembered local authorities are obliged to help all children in need and are working under much greater pressure. The voluntary societies may help whom they choose.

The Coram Foundation for Children finds foster-homes for the first babies of unmarried mothers to give these mothers a 'breathing space' and claims that its arrangements have never broken down. Only serious illness or the death of a foster-parent has caused a child's return.

The Church of England Children's Society board out about 20 per cent of the children they help and less than 5 per cent are ever returned.

Dr. Barnardo's board out about 25 per cent of the children in their care and the failure rate for white foster-children in 1965 was 5 per cent among the under-sixes, and 14 per cent of children over ten. More coloured foster-children were returned under six (9 per cent) but fewer over ten (10 per cent). One explanation suggested for this is that more coloured children are totally abandoned and so, once they settle into a foster-home, they are more often left there undisturbed by natural parents.

The motives which impel people to foster children are many and usually mixed. Gordon Trasler[8] lists the more common reasons as: a need for a new emotional relationship; the satisfaction of giving happiness to an unfortunate child; the prestige which possession of children can sometimes bestow; and companionship, for wife (or widow) or for an only child.

The wish to provide a brother or sister for an only child is natural enough, but the foster-child's acceptance in the home may be conditional upon success in a role he is particularly unsuited to play, because an insecure child always finds it difficult to accept a rival for affection. If the child is wanted solely as a companion for the foster-mother she may become unreasonably possessive and fussy in her relationship to the child. A children's officer in Sheffield, Neil Kay, believes two principal motives prompt foster-parents to accept children for long periods. There are those who urgently want a child, or another child, of their own but are unable or unwilling to conceive one; and others who identify closely with deprived children because of memories of deprivation in their own childhood. (An adoption worker at Barnardo's told me they were unlikely to accept foster-parents in this last category because they still had too many problems of their own.)

Miss D. M. Dyson, who has worked many years with Dr. Barnardo's, writes[9] that the desire to gather kudos, to emulate neighbours, to ease a guilty conscience or to satisfy a personal need for someone on whom to lavish affection are among the motives that are not likely to be helpful.

Motives are never likely to be simple, or single, but I can see nothing objectionable about some of the alleged motivations for fostering. Surely there is nothing wrong in a generous desire to share, and the last-mentioned need for someone to love is both a commonplace and commendable desire. Life is, in fact, pointless without the opportunity to love and to be loved. Some of the psychological motives imputed to foster-parents are far-fetched in the extreme. One psychiatrist is on record[10] as saying that a principal motive for fostering was the wish to avoid breast-feeding. This sounds improbable in view of the fact that bottle-feeding is a widespread and acceptable practice today, and no mother is compelled to breast-feed. Indeed she is probably in the minority if she does.

It is often, and rightly, contended that a child in need of a long-stay foster-home is generally a short-stay case which has been mishandled. Moreover, the majority of short-stay cases should not be taken into care at all, but found temporary refuge among relatives, friends, or neighbours. Preventing a child coming into care is half the battle to avoid an emergency becoming a protracted affair and the possibility of the child being left in care indefinitely.

It is almost incredible that nearly 10,000 children a year are taken into care while mother is having another baby; and that another 17,000 children are admitted because of a mother's short illness.[11] This startling evidence of a heartless community is blamed on a number of social factors: greater mobility of families, the character of new housing areas, and a lazy reliance on the Welfare State. Short-term fostering by relatives, friends, or neighbours would overcome the worst danger surrounding the taking of children from their homes, the prospect of their being left in care indefinitely.

John Bowlby points out:[12] 'Some less responsible parents are content to let things slide, and, if the case is neglected long enough, come to adapt their way of life to the absence of the children, making conditions increasingly difficult for the child's return. Other parents, of the more simple-minded kind, are impressed by the generous material conditions in which the children are placed and modestly feel they are better off where they are. . . . This attitude, it must be admitted, is sometimes encouraged by societies, whose pride in the services they render may blind them to the vital need of the child for a continuous intimate relationship which it is so difficult to provide outside his own home circle.'

Of course, it is a better solution for children to be boarded with relatives rather than being taken into care or found foster-homes with complete strangers. Children who go to relatives, however remote the relationship, have an easier entry to membership of the family and the psychological asset of old tribal patterns reasserted. Sometimes the difficulty in the way of the relatives acting is purely financial. This is recognized and under English law a relative may officially register as a foster-parent of one of his young relatives and be paid.

Also, Barnardo's and many other agencies operate cash-grant schemes which encourage relatives to keep the children in their homes, with the help of other practical assistance and guidance from a child-care officer. This voluntary aid can be critical in some cases and the more welcome because of that. For example, if the mother, or relative, is receiving social security allowances, she may only receive £1 a week direct grant without affecting her assistance money, but much practical help can be given in other ways, by gifts of clothing, prams, bedding, and so on. Contributions may be made to the cost of bicycles, fares to hospital, radios for sick children. Then again holiday schemes can be arranged.

Barnardo's also run a Family Assistance Plan which allows for money and other help when there is a reasonably good home in existence but a temporary crisis threatens its security. This society also attempts to rehabilitate problem families by accommodating them all for some months and giving instruction on wise budgeting, child care, housekeeping, and employment prospects. The National Children's Home operate a comparable scheme, and the Church of England Children's Society helps nearly a thousand children in their own homes or in foster-homes financed by them but found by the child's mother. The children's departments of local authorities are beginning to take much greater initiative in such enterprises but preventive work is still woefully underdeveloped. The provision of the most promising foster-home for a deprived child is merely the beginning of the problem. Effective foster-care depends a great deal on the guidance and help available to foster-parents. Most urgently, they need to be prepared unsentimentally for the behaviour a foster-child is likely to show. Because of the pressure to find foster-parents there may be anxiety not to discourage those who seem suitable, but this is a short-sighted policy. Foster-parents who are taken fully into the confidence of the caseworker about the child and his natural parents are far more likely to show maturity and understanding instead of succumbing to a despair which might lead them to ask for the child's removal.

It is insufficiently understood by foster-parents that foster-children are invariably difficult children. Most of them have suffered unhappy experiences, and many have known the impersonal emptiness of institutional life. Separation from parents is often the source of anxieties in the child which can be a crippling handicap in establishing new relationships, particularly with 'parent-substitutes', and many such children are shuffled in and out of a chain of foster-homes. Foster-children need to know about their natural parents, as do adopted children, and need help in understanding their past experiences and the reasons for their parents' inability to look after them. The problem does not disappear if ignored; it becomes a barrier to the close and trusting relationship it is hoped to create between the child and the foster-parents.

When appeals for foster-parents are too indiscriminately addressed, and too unspecific about the children to be fostered, they are likely to fail. The Curtis Committee[13] was told that advertising for foster-homes did not bring good results because a large number of the homes offered proved unsuitable after investigation. The interesting exception to this experience was in one county borough where an advertisement had asked merely for a kind home for a homeless child with no mention of any payment. The replies to this had been uniformly good. One foster-mother who was happily settled with a difficult boy of five told the member who visited her that she had not the least idea when she replied that she would be paid for looking after him. However, the money motive should not be disregarded. Fostering is an ancient tradition and a working-class one. Women have always taken in children like washing to make ends meet. With children they do it for love as well as for money. The cash return is not much but where there are already children any addition to the family income helps the budget. As for love, the working class demonstrates greater affection and tolerance for all children, not just their own.

I

Unfortunately they often harbour the feeling that a legal relationship with somebody else's child, as in adoption, is unnatural, even 'dangerous'. It ignores the strength of the 'blood-tie' and gambles on 'heredity', a subject which attracts many deeply-embedded superstitions. It is probable too, that the working class may be more easily put off adoption by the fancy requirements of the societies and the legal procedure.

I do not believe that pay plays a large part in influencing the success or failure of a foster-home, but it could play a major role in both recruitment and in making clear the modern function of foster-parents. A convention of fostering has long been that foster-parents should be reimbursed, but not rewarded. It was considered, and the view is widely held to this day, that any profit element would attract the wrong people with appalling results for the children. John Bowlby ridicules the argument:[14] 'To fear that paying the foster-mother will affect the natural affection and concern she has for children is as absurd as believing that one's doctor or dentist is less interested in his patient if he may expect to be paid for his services.' Miss D. M. Dyson also wrote:[15] 'It may be that a would-be foster-mother must make some money somehow; and if she would be a good foster-mother if she could afford not to earn, the need to earn will not make her less good.'

Allowances have, in fact, steadily increased, not only to follow the rising cost of living but as an incentive and an acknowledgement of the growing professional relationship between social agency and foster-parents. The old-fashioned foster-mother provided food, physical care, discipline, and instruction in return for the boarding-out allowance. Of course, many of them showed extraordinary love and understanding as well, but this was regarded as their own concern and not that of the agency or caseworker. Today the foster-mother is coming to be regarded more as a partner in a professional job of work. Better pay is linked with the problem of organizing foster care and the idea that foster-parents should be paid to become part of the organization, to be used much as if they were employees, is gaining acceptance.

About ten years ago Dr. Barnardo's Homes decided to pay special allowances to women who needed to earn but preferred to do so by having foster-children. In addition to normal boarding-out allowances for each child there is a retaining payment for each bed, whether occupied or not. This enables women undertaking the care of three or more children to receive a fee in addition to the allowances without the complication which could arise if the same amounts were paid as salaries. In return these foster-mothers undertake to receive the children selected by the Homes without conditions about length of stay, relatives' visits, the child's colour, or such difficulties as bed-wetting. This scheme has made it possible to provide foster-homes for many children who could not easily have been placed, and for families of three or more children to be kept together. Other charities and some local authorities now pay similar retainers to ensure foster-homes are available to babies and children admitted for short periods. A number of local authorities have gone so far as to close down residential nurseries and now rely upon short-term foster-mothers and occasional help from the voluntary societies.

Another recent Barnardo's experiment, to be copied by local authorities, are rent-free houses for professional foster-parents. The couples who accept the service tenancies agree to receive a 'family' of any four to six children chosen for them. These children do not have to face any of the difficulties of assimilation into an ordinary home: they are the home. Nevertheless, the difference between this arrangement and children in a small 'Home' with hired house-parents is a fine one.

Payments for foster-children are fixed independently by the local authorities. The amounts vary from one area to another, but the differences are not considerable. (Examples of the full scale of payments are set out in Appendix A.) Payments to foster-parents by voluntary societies tend to be lower than the rates fixed by local councils, but wherever the money comes from, the boarding-out allowance is about a quarter of the cost of keeping a child in residential care.

There are, of course, private foster-parents. The mother usually finds them and pays them herself. Unless the arrangement is for less than a month, she is legally required to inform the local authority who will then supervise the home as a foster-home; but these private foster-parents do not have to be approved before they receive the child, and supervision can easily be avoided. All that is necessary to evade the law is to send the child away from the home for a day or two before the end of each month, or to find a new foster-mother. Sometimes these foster-mothers are kept waiting for their money and themselves decide that the child must go. In a number of such cases some local authorities take over the payments and then seek reimbursement from the natural mothers.

Until recent years it was hoped that ideally a foster-home would be the place where a deprived child would find all the love and care he needed until he was grown-up. The voluntary societies in England were boarding out children in their care long before the local authorities; but they often made the inhuman mistake of recalling their foster-children into the institutions for training. Little or no effort was made to keep contact with the child's own relatives or to encourage them to have the child back. Children were sent long distances from their former homes and often to areas of declining prosperity where many families were glad of the maintenance payments as a small addition to their incomes.

Gradually attitudes have changed, until now it is fashionable to recognize the importance of the child's relatives and work towards his return to them as soon as possible. Parents are encouraged to visit and to keep in close touch. Both foster-children and foster-parents are advised to regard their relationship as impermanent if not temporary.

According to Miss D. M. Dyson, it was largely the children themselves who prompted this change of policy. She wrote:[16] 'In many cases children who had lost all touch with their families during schooldays insisted on being put in touch with them again in adolescence: this insistence both showed their need of their relations and led to the discovery that many had satisfactory relations who were only too glad to meet them and sometimes to have them home, so that all concerned came to appreciate the right of the child and of the relations to maintain contact, and the unnecessary suffering caused by failure to do so.'

This appears both emotionally and intellectually sound, but when most foster-care was long-term, foster-parents fulfilled a parental role, largely unchallenged by the child's own parents or by the possibility of his eventual removal. Reunion with his family was unlikely and the child frequently used the foster-parents' name. Now, with the aim of rehabilitating the natural family and the expansion of short-term care, foster-parents are discouraged from identifying with the child to the same extent, and it is made clear to them that theirs is not the parental role but a caretaking job.

It is not surprising that many who long to fulfil the old roles of foster-parents are not interested in the new interpretation. The changes have been directed from the best of motives and to protect everybody's rights and interests. Only the children have been robbed.

Unfortunately, the truth remains that young children need parents, not caretakers. They cannot be happy as lodgers; they must 'belong'. Modern foster-mothers are being asked to do the impossible, to 'mother' at arm's length, to love without commitment.

NOTES

1. Report of the Care of Children Committee (The Curtis Committee) (H.M.S.O. 1946).

2. 18 May 1967.

3. Mr. Leo Abse, the Labour M.P. for Pontypool, is an advocate for such a reform, and suggests a three-year limit before loss of parental rights if parents fail to provide a home of their own.

4. Yarrow, L. J., 'Research in Dimensions of Early Maternal Care' in *Merrill-Palmer Quarterly*, **9**, 101–14 (1963).

5. Trasler, Gordon, *In Place of Parents* (Routledge & Kegan Paul, 1960).

6. Parker, R. A., *Decision in Child Care* (George Allen & Unwin Ltd., 1966).

7. Dyson, D. M., *No Two Alike* (George Allen & Unwin Ltd., 1962).

8. Trasler, Gordon, *In Place of Parents* (Routledge & Kegan Paul, 1960).

9. Dyson, D. M., *No Two Alike* (George Allen & Unwin Ltd., 1962).

10. *Case Conference*, June 1966 issue.

11. Figures taken from 'Children in Care in England and Wales', March 1967, H.M.S.O.

12. Bowlby, John, *Child Care and the Growth of Love* (Penguin Books, 1965).

13. Report of the Care of Children Committee (The Curtis Committee) (H.M.S.O., 1946).

14. Bowlby, John, *Child Care and the Growth of Love* (Penguin Books, 1965).

15. Dyson, D. M., *No Two Alike* (George Allen & Unwin Ltd., 1962).

16. Ibid.

9

Sex

Two reasons why a township of illegitimate babies are born each year in this country are a lack of realistic sex education to counter the driving commercial exploitation of sex in our society and the earlier physical maturation of youth. A third reason tragically gives the problem of illegitimacy an internal momentum of its own and cuts across barriers of age and upbringing. This is the lack of love in the lives of many of those who become un-married parents, a deprivation which often makes them incapable of loving their own children, who, in turn, become single parents, or if married, inadequate and neglectful.

The number of illegitimate births in this country has more than doubled in the past ten years. In 1966 the figure totalled 67,056 and the large majority of bastards (42,575) were born to women under twenty-four. Of these young unmarried mothers 20,582 were teenagers, and 21,993 between the ages of twenty and twenty-four; but, surprisingly, more than a third of the total (23,481) were women aged from twenty-five to forty-nine.

I do not wish here to make ethical judgements or to offer either condonations or condemnations. I do not find any concept of absolute moral values useful and prefer to consider ideas of right and wrong in relation to subjective evaluations, dependent upon individual personalities and particular circumstances. To this extent I am at odds with the many to whom immorality would still seem to mean but one thing: sex outside marriage, which they consider is 'absolutely' wrong.

This rigid attitude in support of chastity has considerable appeal to those who are opposed to the liberality, or licence, permitted in sexual relationships within present-day society, and to those who by conviction, or from expediency, find that only black and white standards of morality allow any security of dogma or conscience for a teacher, parson, or parent.

Such an attitude, however, fails to take any account of changes since the times of Jesus and Paul, and of the theological, social, and moral problems these inevitably pose. The mass of young people in Western countries are no longer prepared to run their sex lives in accord with the edicts of the Christian Churches. Most girls are now physically mature by the time they are thirteen and young men at the peak of their virility in their late teens. The notion that it is right to regard developing sexuality as a matter for inflexible discipline and self-control can be attacked as a denial of valuable experience, if not the deliberate arrest of normal development. It is also arguable that sexual maturity demands sexual experience and that the rejection of the sex act until marriage is not the way to discover its rightful use in our lives. I believe that young people should be taught to criticize, to question, and to form their own independent judgements. I am convinced, too, that their own personally thought-out morality is the least likely to collapse under the powerful pressures of modern advertising and the new drives towards a mindless conformity within a society that is placing an unprecedented value upon youth and teenage cults.

The biggest challenge of the illegitimacy problem lies in breaking the vicious circle of deprived children becoming parents (single or married) of a new generation of children who will be equally incapable of making satisfactory human relationships which will last. The negative wish not to have an illegitimate child 'because I was one and know all about it' is not enough: there must be the more positive creative wish to make a good home and become loving parents, to seek and secure a quality of life. As I have said earlier, a positive attitude towards the responsibility of parenthood has its real roots in a warm and secure family life.

Such a background should also play an important part in helping young people to ensure that they make conscious, if not considered, decisions about sex. The excuse, 'I don't know what came over me, it just happened' must be outlawed as irresponsible and ridiculous when offered for an unwanted baby.

Sex must not be regarded as a capricious fantasy divorced from reality which renders the mind and will inert and powerless. Too many young people blind themselves to the fact that they are having sexual intercourse either because they are living in a dream world manufactured for the mass media or because they are extraordinarily ignorant. Intercourse seems unreal until later. Unfortunately, as yet there is no retroactive birth control pill for swallowing the morning after.

Another difficulty is that the level of communication between many young people is frequently so inadequate that they cannot talk about methods of birth control or the use of them. At the heart of a great many unwelcome situations in which young people find themselves is an unthinking and unrealistic attitude towards sex. Michael Schofield's recent research[1] into the sexual behaviour of a sample of nearly 2,000 teenagers found that less than half the boys always used contraceptives and a quarter never used them. The girls usually left it to the boys with the result that the majority neither used contraceptives themselves nor insisted that their partners did. The possibility of pregnancy was never considered by some, and others admitted that they refused to allow themselves to be worried by the possibility. Forty per cent of the boys were untroubled by the prospect of making the girl pregnant.

Another researcher[2] who interviewed a more promiscuous group of teenagers found that only 17 per cent practised birth control. Quite a large group in this sample did not like contraceptives or could not be bothered with them. The most usual birth control method was either the sheath or withdrawal; but some of the boys who possessed sheaths had not had intercourse and had bought them as a status symbol.

In spite of our much publicized 'permissive society' not all young people now have sex before marriage but a large minority do.[3] This appetite for sexual experience is openly encouraged by the commercial engineers of the teenage cult, the creators of sex symbols for the wider exploitation of the teenage market of money and emotions. Unfortunately, the power of the erotic incitement generated by this style of commerce has not been sufficiently recognized as more than enough justification for frank and fearless sex education. As a result, young people are the more inclined to sexual experimentation and the more vulnerable to misadventure.

There is much freer discussion about sexual matters but it is seldom carried on between adults and children with the maturity and understanding required for real communication across the growing gulf between the generations. Many young people are never invited to talk about sex at school or at home, nor do some of them feel free to do so. The majority first learn how babies are born from their friends. Usually through jokes. Schofield's research shows that by twelve or thirteen most children know, or think they know, the facts of life. Much of this information comes from their friends and much is inaccurate and crude. Unhappily, when informed sex education comes later these children are often disinclined to listen because they think they know it all, and the misunderstandings and prejudices which have taken root early remain.

Among Schofield's group two-thirds of the boys and a quarter of the girls had learnt nothing about sex from their parents. Even those who had discussed sex at home had usually first heard about it from another source. When parental advice about sex was offered it was unspecific and vague and usually concentrated on moral problems. Middle-class daughters were the most likely to be helped by their mothers and working-class sons the least likely to learn about sex from either parent. Few boys had learnt about sex from their mothers and only 7 per cent of them had heard anything about conception from their fathers. Another 7 per cent had found out from books.

In some countries sex education in schools is forbidden because it is held that parents are the proper people to instruct the children. Schofield's research suggests that this is unlikely to work well in practice. He writes: 'Even when special classes are instituted to help the parents to teach their children about sex the people who attend classes are probably ones who would have talked to their children about sex in any case.'

This may well be a serious difficulty but it is one well worth tackling. Some parents react emotionally against talking about the subject, but the main reason so many working-class parents will not talk to their children about sex is that they literally cannot find the words. It is doubtful whether they could give a coherent and correct explanation of the sexual act to anyone, let alone a mystified child. Description of menstruation, seminal emission and birth are even further beyond them.

One group of nine mothers under sixteen[4] said that their mothers had told them practically nothing about menstruation and pregnancy. The pitiable inadequacy of the communication between mother and daughter is illustrated by the few phrases the girls could recollect. 'You start bleeding, that means you are a woman, or that you can have a baby' . . . 'don't let a boy do anything to you'.

A girl expecting an illegitimate baby described her feelings on radio:[5] 'I am so ashamed for my parents because I have had such a good home. . . .' Asked whether her parents had ever discussed sex with her, she replied, quite shocked at the idea: 'Oh no, we never talked about things like that . . . I was well brought up.' She herself had been illegitimate and was adopted.

The widespread ignorance, confusion, and embarrassment surrounding sex must be dispelled among many parents if they are to help their children in any meaningful way. There is no substitute for the help of mature loving parents in this or any other role, and children will listen to their parents about sex if only they make sense of it!

Schools appear to be more concerned to give sex education to girls than to boys: 86 per cent of the girls in Schofield's study had received some formal sex education at school, compared with less than 50 per cent of the boys. Most of the girls received biological and physiological instruction. Some were also given moral advice but few received any technical information. Also, the amount of sex education given to girls did not seem to vary among different types of schools. On the other hand, among boys those in private schools are the most likely to be given sex education: 71 per cent of boys from private schools had received some sex instruction, and for one in three of them this included technical information about reproduction and a description of sexual intercourse. The State-educated boys seldom received anything more than biological and physiological instruction without any discussion of intercourse.

Nearly half the boys and girls were dissatisfied with both the quantity and quality of the sex education they received at school. Most of them thought it important for a person who gives sex education to have had some first-hand experience of sex, which appears fair comment. Unfortunately Schofield's survey of nearly 2,000 teenagers is disappointing when it tries to assess the quality of the instruction. One girl quoted in the report says: 'A teacher tried once; he started on about frogs, but after he had said about three lines on tadpoles and the fellows all laughed, he packed it in.' Another girl said that there was only one lesson 'with a young mistress where we asked questions like was it right to have it before marriage'.

Many schools, however, do provide useful sex education within a broadly-based syllabus of discussions about personal relationships, feelings, and attitudes. Predictably, many teenagers will reject adult advice of all kinds, but a redeeming feature of teenage society is their passion for discussion, particularly of human problems. Teenagers are anxious for sex education if it is given with authority and a proper understanding of their problems.[6]

The difficulty even in an enlightened situation lies in the no-man's-land between the moral frontiers of different generations. Contemporary public attitudes towards casual sex are becoming neutral but those who draw up syllabuses for sex education, however liberal, are unlikely to condone fornication even when contraception is used.

During lessons on sex in secondary schools in Gloucestershire,[7] children are told that sexual intercourse implies 'total committal', is 'basically for reproduction', and 'has a place only in marriage where a secure home can be made for the children'. All these statements are highly debatable,[8] and young people will reach their own personal conclusions.

Even some churchmen no longer believe chastity should

be the inflexible rule of conduct outside marriage. The report of the British Council of Churches working party on sex[9] concluded that people should be 'led to an understanding of sex which would enable them to make up their own minds'. The report held that rules by themselves are an inadequate basis for morality, and no rule can cover all the varied and complex situations in which men and women find themselves. The dilemma of the Churches is reflected in the homes, where the quality and extent of the advice proffered by parents varies considerably. Schofield's report quotes one parent who merely told her daughter, 'no one wants soiled goods', and another mother who instructed her daughter on the use of contraceptives.

The truth is that despite some efforts by parents, teachers, and clergymen in matters of sex young people are principally instructed by their peers. As a result, a satisfactory response to the boy friend's love-making is often considered more important than using reliable contraception.

This order of priorities is, I believe, truly immoral, for implicit in such an attitude is unconcern about producing an unwanted baby. This is the situation which sex education should seek above all to avoid.

It is an appalling social indictment that in the last fifteen years there has been at least a 300 per cent increase in the total number of births to girls under eighteen and that many of these young girls may well have felt offended if offered contraceptives. A group of pregnant schoolgirls told one psychiatrist[10] who interviewed them that they felt instruction in the use of contraceptives not only would have been an insult, but an incitement to sexual behaviour. One girl said that their mothers would not have thought much of them if they had considered putting them 'on the pill' at puberty. She was unshaken when another girl commented, 'They would have been right, wouldn't they?'

Contraception alone will not solve the problem of illegitimacy: the techniques must be accompanied by explanation and discussion; and, above all, a sense of realism and personal onus about their behaviour must be awakened in the young and the sexually footloose. Many people claim that contraception will not dramatically lower the illegitimacy rate, and the fact that contraceptives are commonly used is bound to produce more 'accidents'. More girls having sex means more girls are vulnerable to bearing an illegitimate baby.

It is also widely held by psychiatrists that many girls, and some boys, need a baby as a love-object, or as a proof of fecundity. Again, many boys and girls, particularly those from deprived homes, need evidence of their own lovability, while others are bedevilled by more complicated feelings; an urge for self-punishment or to revolt against harsh parents.

Sweden is commonly cited as an example of a socially enlightened country where contraceptives are freely available and where the illegitimacy rate is much higher than ours. The other side of the picture is less emphasized. The growth of sex education in Sweden since the nineteen-thirties and the deliberate spread of knowledge about more effective methods of birth control, nearly halved the number of illegitimate births between 1930 and 1950.[11]

Now, at last, there are signs that new attitudes are freshening the old moralistic climate of veto and secrecy which used to surround contraception in this country. Since 1963 the Brook Advisory Centres[12] have been carrying out the twofold tasks of counselling the young and unmarried on their emotional and sexual problems and instructing them in contraception. In 1967 the two London clinics saw 3,253 new patients, compared with 2,236 in 1966. About a third of the girls were students and the rest came from many walks of life. The largest number of patients are twenty to twenty-one, and women over twenty-five were referred to the Marie Stopes Centre. The London Brook clinics now have a waiting list of six to eight weeks.

Branches are open in Birmingham, Harlow, Cambridge, Edinburgh and Liverpool. The latest is at Bristol, where the illegitimate birth rate has risen to $10\frac{1}{2}$ per cent and nearly doubled in the past five years.

One of the most important changes in our attitude towards sex is expressed in the National Health Service (Family Planning) Bill which became law in June 1967. The Bill gives local authorities the power to make contraceptives available to all, and soon after it reached the Statute Book, the Family Planning Association, which now has 770 birth control clinics, began to open them to anyone over sixteen, whether married or not. The Association's new policy now applies to about 400 clinics. There are already long waiting-lists at its clinics[13] and the rate at which services are developed will depend a great deal upon local feeling and the support of local councils. More than 90 per cent of clinics are rented from local authorities but as yet only 26 out of 204 Local Health Authorities have indicated that they will provide a full family planning service through the F.P.A.

Nevertheless, local authorities are in a more difficult position to protest now that they themselves are free to organize these services, and may even be directed by the Minister of Health to do so. Contraceptive advice, the Bill directs, should be given on medical and social grounds and there is no distinction made between the married and unmarried. Previously, local authorities were urged to provide this service only for medical reasons; but what are the new grounds and who will decide them?

Already there is apprehension among the more experienced and sensitive practitioners in this field that it will be years before the clinics envisaged by the Bill can be established and staffed with doctor/counsellors trained in the sexual and emotional problems of the young and unmarried. In the meantime, all that is likely to be given will be straightforward instruction in contraception.

The difference between merely offering birth control advice with contraceptives and combining this with professional counselling for young people is the fuel for a new controversy about the principles involved. Brook began work with the young and the unmarried under the direct supervision of a medical director, Dr. Faith Spicer. Three years later the doctor resigned, saying that in important medical spheres she had been supplanted by lay workers, and that help with emotional problems was as necessary as practical instruction in contraception.

Brook Centres maintain that their methods are unchanged. Extra time for discussion and help in emotional difficulties is always available, and other agencies are used when necessary.

Twice-weekly sessions are now run for those girls with special problems, when each girl is given a fifty-minute consultation. Sir Theodore Fox, a former member of the Board of Brook Centres and former Director of the Family Planning Association, has claimed:[14] 'The present controversy has polarized differences of opinion, but the two parties are much nearer than they appear. In real life nobody thinks that *every* girl requires lengthy counselling, and nobody thinks that *any* girl should have contraceptives on demand.'

I disagree with Sir Theodore. Most girls do need to talk over this matter in depth with a sympathetic and qualified counsellor, and, as every girl is liable to have sexual intercourse, every girl should have easy access to contraceptives. It is also highly relevant to point out that of the girls who consult Brook, 10 per cent have had an illegitimate child or an abortion.[15] The founder of the organization, Helen Brook, also told me they have rarely fitted a girl who is a virgin.

The British Council of Churches Working Party's report 'Sex and Morality' places such importance on counselling as a vital part of contraceptive advice for the unmarried that it suggests the community should be prepared to pay the cost of ensuring this is available.

The working party also endorsed two strictures laid down by Dr. Alex Comfort. These are that in free love precaution should be taken to avoid producing an unwanted child, and there should be no exploitation of another's feelings. Excellent rules. But is it possible to keep the second? Even the report expressed doubts: 'It is in the nature of the experience that you don't know what it is going to be, for yourself or the other person; you certainly cannot count on its being the same for both and ending conveniently at the same moment. So what is an agreeable recreation for the one may be a consuming fire for the other.'

Obviously girls are more vulnerable in premarital sexual relations than their boy friends from practical, emotional, and social considerations. Many girls run the risk of pregnancy—most of Schofield's teenage girls did—and if they conceive they are lucky to get any help from the father. Emotionally the girl usually looks for a romantic relationship and the boy for sexual experience. The girl wants security, the boy adventure. Socially, men having sex are indulging legitimately in 'a good time', women are 'making themselves cheap'. British upbringing does not encourage boys to behave responsibly about their sexuality. They start off badly: few parents talk to their sons about sex, and most boys' schools ignore the subject or introduce it too late.

With absurd lack of realism, girls still leave 'precautions' in sex to their boy friends. More often than not the boys do not bother: unprepared and unconcerned, they do not begin to understand the stupidity and cruelty of causing an unwanted baby to be born. It is encouraging, however, that some boys accompany their girl-friends to the Brook clinics and a few are consulting the centres themselves for advice on sexual and psychological matters. The National Council for the Unmarried Mother and Her Child also reports that a number of unmarried fathers now seek their advice. Some make inquiries on the mother's behalf, some ask for advice on maintenance payments and some ask for information on pregnancy tests. In 1966–7 four fathers sought help in establishing a claim to their illegitimate child.

It is common in Sweden for unmarried mothers to announce births in newspapers and for the schoolgirl mother to become a romanticized figure, with classmates happily knitting for the new arrival. In this country unmarried mothers do not, as yet, advertise the baby's arrival, but a half-amused and half-indulgent acceptance has crept in for the bastard of a celebrity. A well-known writer, actress, artist, or entertainer may have a bastard and find the child adds to the glamour surrounding them. 'She's a wonderful mother really. . . .' 'It's a cute little thing. . . .' 'She's got a gem of a nanny. . . .' 'When she comes back from the States she's laden with presents for the lucky child. . . .'

Strangely, there are few research studies of the effects of paternal deprivation but, obviously, fathers are important. A man's economic and emotional support is necessary if a mother is fully to enjoy her baby. The young boy who fails to identify with a loved father or father-substitute is more likely to develop homosexual tendencies and will lack any example on which to

K

base his future roles as husband and father. A girl's father will help to form and influence her attitude towards men; and equally important is her observation of the father's relationship with her mother.

The sexual precocity of some of Schofield's teenagers was related to the amount of parental discipline. Lack of it accounted for much staying out too late, and for petting parties which got out of hand. Half the sexually experienced in Schofield's sample had been drunk three or more times in their own estimation, and only a few had never thought themselves drunk.

Adolescents do not want to be 'trusted' too soon, and parents still exert the strongest influence upon their children's development. If sex is to be enjoyed and the numbers of illegitimate babies reduced, helping parents to talk to their children about sex is more important than improving sex instruction at school, for this often comes too late and with a prudish academic emphasis on biological facts rather than techniques and passions.

It is far from easy to provide effective but aesthetic sex education within the home or school and well-financed large-scale campaigns are needed to begin to offset the effects of mass advertising which sells sex along with a pop song or a brand of soap. Again, easier said than achieved; but pilot schemes could begin now to make it the smart thing to use Brook, socially to ostracize those who want sex so irresponsibly that they cannot even bother to learn and practise contraception.

It is not only teenagers who are distressingly ignorant and impulsive: thousands of illegitimate babies are born to older women. In 1966 women over thirty produced 11,630 bastards. Many women feel life is passing them by and are grateful enough for a chance of sex to be careless of precautions. More than 600 women over forty became unmarried mothers in 1966, some perhaps falsely fortified by a belief that their ages were against any likelihood of conception. Such is the state of ignorance and recklessness that men and women of all ages could be greatly helped towards a maturer understanding of sex.

NOTES

1. Schofield, Michael, *The Sexual Behaviour of Young People* (Longmans, Green, 1965).

2. Ponting, L. I., 'The Social Aspects of Venereal Disease among Young People in Leeds and London,' *Brit. J.Ven.Dis.* **39**, 273–7 (1963).

3. Michael Schofield estimates that more than 350,000 boys and girls under twenty have had experience of premarital intercourse.

4. Anderson, E. W. *et al.*, 'Psychiatric, Social and Psychological Aspects of Illegitimate Pregnancy in Girls under Sixteen Years' (*Psychiat. et Neurol.*, 207–220 Basel, 1957).

5. 'Focus on Illegitimacy,' BBC Home Service, 4 April 1967.

6. The National Marriage Guidance Council runs courses to share with teachers the approach it has found useful in helping young people individually and in groups.

7. Regarded as a model series and described in detail in *Family Doctor*, March 1966.

8. As long ago as 1955, Geoffrey Gorer in *Exploring British Character* found that only about half the men and 63 per cent of the women in his large sample of all ages disapproved of premarital sex.

9. *Sex and Morality*, a report to the British Council of Churches (S.C.M. Press, 1966).

10. Dr. Donald Gough on 'The Very Young Mother' at a conference on 'Pregnancy in Adolescence', organized by the N.C.U.M.C. on 10 March 1966.

11. The rate fell from 16 per cent to 9·5 per cent, and fewer girls were pregnant upon marriage.

12. Brook, a registered charity, had received £20,000 by May 1967, including £15,000 from a friend of Helen Brook, the founder, given 'out of compassion for unwanted babies'. Clients are charged £3 a year which covers any number of visits; they also pay for any supplies required. In cases of hardship fees are waived. Since 1964, 10,000 young people have been helped. An appeal for funds is now being launched so that more advisory centres may be opened.

13. In 1966, 128,000 new clients were seen.

14. He wrote a letter to *The Observer*, 28 February 1967.

15. Brook Centres 1966 report.

10

Rejected Adopters

ADOPTION agencies have lived for too long in a state of complacency engendered and nourished by a past in which there were ten would-be adopters anxious for every homeless child. As a result adoption workers assumed a God-like role in discharging their duties. They selected 'ideal parents'; they sought for them children of 'matching characteristics'. Now supply and demand has changed dramatically, many adoption societies in this country still cling to their arbitrary rules and outworn attitudes. It is a comfortable contemporary myth that there are today more prospective adopters than there are children without parents. In fact, there is a surplus of children and a shortage of parents. Even for white healthy babies of good background there is no longer a super-abundance of adopters; and, if thousands more children are offered for adoption despite handicaps of religion, age, colour and health, the position will be seen to be scandalous. Passive acceptance of traditional methods and an innate capacity to ignore a problem once it has been delegated to a tangle of voluntary and statutory committees enables this crisis to remain submerged in England.

American agencies faced with a similarly changed adoption situation have already reshaped their ideas. Happily it is now realized in the United States that the risk to a child of what appears to be a poor home is far less than the danger of no home at all. The effect of America's radical reappraisal is that their assessments of applicants and children are more flexible and the child's urgent need now dictates American adoption policy. Couples are no longer turned down almost automatically because of middle age, a divorce, no formal religion or a low income. Nor are they refused because they have their own children.

As part of the research for this book I wrote to the English press asking rejected adopters to get in touch with me. The *Sun*, the *New Statesman* and the *Spectator* published my letter and I also advertised once in the personal columns of the *Daily Telegraph* and the *New Statesman*. The total response was fifty to sixty letters recounting unhappy and frustrating experiences in attempting to adopt children.

All these letters suggest that misguided caution, ignorance, and even arrogance, are robbing many children of parents and many couples of children. Of course, those who wrote may be guilty of exaggeration, distortion, even misrepresentation; but too much of what they say rings true to be disregarded. Some letters show poor education and are badly expressed; others are highly literate. Many are idealistic and all of them come from the heart. Almost without exception they reveal degrees of courage and good-humoured patience which are humbling. Some say they have written reluctantly, their memories are painful. There are no names and addresses here for obvious reasons. Some who wrote are still trying to adopt children and all believe that by relating their experiences they might help to create a deeper understanding of the need for reforms which will make the adoption procedures more logical, dignified and human.

'*It is no use being an ideal adoptive parent if you can't actually adopt . . . Somehow the continual encouragement and assurances of what marvellous adoptive parents we would make from friends, health visitors, doctors and teachers, far from being a help, in the end just made me feel like laughing hollowly.*'

London housewife

'*We were told there was nothing against our characters in any way. We passed medicals, we had good references and our home was visited and was found satisfactory. But after the board meeting we received a letter saying our application had been turned down. We was bitterly disappointed as we could have given the baby a good home and all the love and care our little boy would of had.'*

> Roman Catholic couple,[1] own child of four killed in a motor accident a year before

'For the past four years we have approached innumerable adoption societies and have merely acquired a large and saddening file of refusals. We are now having to resign ourselves to a childless life.'

> Jewish schoolteacher married to a surgeon

'Adoption societies don't care for coloured children, they are suspicious of adopters.'

> A rabbi's wife

'We were rejected, probably because I was honest about my religious beliefs. The Society had, it was said, no religious bias. Had I cooked up a story about what I believed, had I been conventional in my attitude to religion I believe we would have been accepted.'

> Teacher (deputy head of an Approved School)

'We should like a family of four but don't feel justified in producing them all ourselves when there is a serious population problem and uncared for children.'

> Teacher's wife

'It's awful to long to give one's love and not be allowed to.'

> Home Counties housewife

'My husband is a postman and we haven't much money but we are a very happy family and I think our adoptions have all been a success yet we would not have had any of our children had we not lied and persevered and the two youngest wouldn't have been adopted at all.'

> Adoptive mother of four, two white and two coloured children

Nearly all of those who wrote complain that no reasons are given for their rejection as adopters. There is also bitterness about unaccountable delays and the offhand attitude of some officials who show small appreciation of the importance of their 'Committee's decision' to the applicants. All would-be adopters steel themselves to be 'investigated', psychologically, socially, and medically. Invariably they put up with delays and uncertainties. At the end all my correspondents got was a short uninformative note of rejection typed in trite official prose. This treatment is resented as unnecessary and childish, even insulting. Imagine the hopes, the waiting, then:

'*Just a brief note saying* we trust you will not take this decision too badly.
'*I did take it badly and tried to contact the adoption officer on the 'phone only to be told she was out of the office all day.*'

Home Counties housewife

'*A Child Care officer visited our home, talked to us at length and left us with the promise that official application forms would be posted on. These did not arrive, so after a week my wife telephoned the department. She was unable to contact the Child Care Officer and although a message was left, the officer did not ring back.*
'*I then wrote to the department and received* a short and evasive letter from which we gathered that we were not considered as suitable applicants.'

Airline captain married to a former
child care Officer

'*After this final interview we were told that our application had now to be considered by the full adoption committee of the Society—a mere formality to confirm the interviewer's agreement to our becoming adoptive parents. My wife was told by the interviewer what to do in preparation.*
'But within a week the letter of rejection reached us. Enquiries from me met, of course, with the expected brick wall.'

Teacher

The effects of rejection upon prospective parents obviously depend to some extent upon the temperament and resilience of the individuals concerned, but for all the experience is deeply hurtful. Some would-be mothers are so distressed that they become mentally and physically ill.

> *'I have had three depressive illnesses although I am well enough to teach in between. This is now another reason for rejection.'*
>
> Jewish teacher

> *'After a great strain and a lot of what seems unnecessary questions, only to be refused is heart-breaking. So long was the wait that my wife had a minor breakdown after the disappointing result.'*
>
> North Country man

> *'The emotional strain involved is fantastic. After our son had arrived safely and we could relax I felt physically ill. I expect he will be an only child because we certainly couldn't go through all this again.'*
>
> Couple who, rejected by adoption agencies in this country, adopted a foreign child privately

> *'Of course I mind our friends and neighbours knowing. They must wonder if there is something* wrong *with us that we are not allowed to have a child.'*
>
> Social worker

It is evident that rejection is made worse by the point-blank nature of refusal. Theoretically, many experts agree the correct way to handle rejections is to save the feelings of the applicants by getting them to withdraw: they should be led to discover for themselves that adoption is not the right course for them. Such theories are nonsense. A child is the heart's desire of these couples. Again, adoption workers are not psychiatrists and have neither the time nor the skill to practise such subtle techniques.

It is often claimed that secrecy must be kept when medical references are unsatisfactory and the doctor will not disclose these reasons to adopters. In my view, doctors should be prepared to discuss problems more realistically with their patients. Possibly there is more relevant need for secrecy when the adoption agency learns of serious criminal offences to which applicants have not admitted. Police inquiries could be justified occasionally as confidential. With this exception the withholding of reasons for refusal is the more often heartless officialdom in action. Reasons for rejection should be given, and in person. Adopters are entitled to know why they have not been found suitable. Letters are inadequate for the purpose because the situation raises doubts about personal integrity and fitness for parenthood. Face-to-face discussion at least allows the release of emotions and provides an opportunity for doubts and fears to be rationalized and placed in perspective. Some adoption workers appear to forget that it is the deep-seated belief of most people that they would make worth-while parents; or that some rejected adopters already have, or will have, children of their own.

> '*After being rejected we waited a year or so and we were just starting to make further enquiries when my wife found herself to be pregnant after eight years of marriage and we now have our own young daughter. Her presence around us serves only to emphasise to us the tragedy of the adoption situation. I feel like asking a representative of the society we approached to visit us again and to tell us why our home is unsuitable for our child.*'
>
> Teacher

Many experts contend there is a difference in the qualities needed for good natural parents and good adoptive parents. The difference is too subtle for a layman to appreciate. Briefly, the argument is that if you reject your own child because he fails to fulfil parental hopes this is a rejection of a part of yourself, but an adopted child is rejected the more easily for personal identification with him is not so deep.

There are adopters too ready to blame an unknown 'heredity'

for all manner of shortcomings but in my opinion this is due in part to the atmosphere of apprehension created by current adoption procedures. The counter-arguments are stronger. The adopted child is not wanted as an 'extension of oneself'. He can enjoy a more relaxed and tolerant relationship for most adopters feel an *extra* sense of responsibility towards an adopted child and are keenly conscious that he must not suffer a repetition of rejection. Also, they are not personally involved in his inheritance, in his turning out a member of the family tribe duly approving characteristics of his forebears. No family traits are looked for or expected. He is wonderfully free to be himself.

Released from vain preconceptions of their children's talents, it is arguable that some adoptive parents are better equipped for their roles than natural parents. Also, they never have a family by accident; or if they live in one room. Frequently, they are more mature than a couple having their first baby. They are likely to be older and more established, and the joint decision to adopt in itself indicates a marriage within which ambitions, fears, and purposes are discussed and shared.

All these considerations make it the more unforgivable that a number of my correspondents were rejected as adopters without even the courtesy of an explanation, and then accepted as long-term foster-parents.

> '*My wife and I have been refused twice by adoption societies. We do not know why. After a great strain, only to be refused is heartbreaking . . . However, we have since been foster-parents to two children. They have now returned to their father and we are waiting for some more.*'

North Country couple

> '*We began writing to adoption agencies which all proved to no avail. My own doctor is baffled at the replies for I may foster but not adopt.*'

North Country housewife

There can be no moral defence for a couple refused the opportunity to adopt a child then being used as foster-parents. This is pure expediency and exploitation, to cloak the indecision and qualms of the social worker. If would-be parents are not considered good enough to adopt, why should they be encouraged to foster? Foster-children, disturbed and rebellious about the early denial of love in their lives, are a far more difficult challenge than young babies needing adoption. Such confusion of thought abounds. The statutory agencies make pressing demands for foster-parents. They are compelled by law to board out children whenever possible and compete to place as many as possible of the children in their care. Voluntary societies too need foster-homes. In the resulting scrimmage of competition essential truths are brushed away. Fostering requires outstanding qualities of character and toughness if an enduring and loving home is to be made for the foster-children. And yet, as the law now stands, these unfortunate children are lodgers without security.

Sometimes it is felt that would-be adopters have many sterling qualities but not enough to succeed in raising children without the support of 'the Department'. Often these couples are persuaded to become foster-parents because all foster-homes are supervised by child care officers. Unfortunately, this outside surveillance undermines their authority with children who have a special need for adult examples of self-reliance and stability. Fostering can place intolerable strains on both parents and children and should certainly not be regarded as suitable second-rate employment for unacceptable adopters.

Even more deplorable perhaps is the practice of hesitant social workers to use foster-children to test the capacities of prospective adopters.

> '*We then heard from the L.C.C. that they would consider us as adopters if we agreed to foster one of their children in care for them to assess us.*'
>
> London couple

The idea is not only absurd and patronizing to the would-be adopters but unfair to the foster-child. For however short a term, he is a 'guinea-pig' in an experiment. He may even be removed peremptorily and for apparently spurious reasons.

> *'Having two sons of our own, we applied for a boy to foster. We were persuaded to take a pair of brothers aged 11 and 14½. We had some trouble with them, particularly the elder who seemed to be on his way to becoming a real tearaway. With the help of a local farmer we got him straight and two visiting officers of the children's department considered us to be first-class foster-parents.*
>
> *'After three years we applied for a girl. A 12 year old was selected. She had been with two families previously and was now in a children's home. She came to us for a series of weekends and we became fond of her and I think she was of us and of our home . . . It was then decided that it was not suitable for her to be in a home with so many males, and apart from one visit we were not allowed to see her again.'*

Yorkshireman

> *'My husband and I have just been through the terrible ordeal of parting with a foster-child after nearly three years. As soon as we applied for adoption the local authorities took her from us and put her in another foster-home. Her own mother didn't want her, she was wanted and loved by us. We were the only mother and father she ever knew. The only excuse they gave us was that she was spoilt and out of control. What did they expect us to do, keep hitting her?'*

Yorkshire housewife

Others experienced the grief of having a child reclaimed by a parent, a stranger to a terrified child who had given its total love and trust to foster-parents.

> *'Just 10½ years after getting our foster daughters we had a letter saying prepare them for going back home in 48 hours. After 10½ years with never a half-day away from us . . .'*

Mr. & Mrs. X

Foster-children and parents must be protected against such blind cruelty. No grossly neglectful parent should be able to reassert rights of possession long after the child has identified deeply with loving substitute parents, and reform of the law to prevent abuse is urgently needed. Such parents are wrongly protected if they bring about such traumatic separations, and grief near to mourning.

It is widely held that couples aged forty to fifty can make admirable foster-parents but if they adopt children they might not be able to cope, financially, physically, or mentally ten years later. Certainly, there is good evidence[2] that women over forty succeed best in fostering. On the other hand, no evidence has been produced to suggest that women of this age make unsatisfactory adoptive mothers. Not surprisingly there are many complaints about the arbitrary age limits applied to would-be adopters.

'I feel the age limit could be altered to 45 at least. Women are not old at 40 years now as in olden days. Many have children even later.'

Midlands housewife

'We waited several months before being told we were too old when we could have been told when we first applied.'

West Country couple

'I was refused a baby because of my age. I don't feel bitter about it as I had a little boy the same year. He is our pride and joy. So you see at the time I was being refused a child I was having my own.'

North Country housewife

'We were told we were too old to adopt a baby but it wasn't suggested we should adopt an older child. We would have been glad to do this.'

Londoners

Adoption officers rationalize their prejudices against older adopters on a number of grounds. The mother is faced with a trying and energetic toddler when she is at the difficult stage of the menopause. The large age difference makes it harder for the parents to tolerate teenage attitudes and behaviour, and at that age children do not like their parents to look more like grandparents. The father will be retiring when the children reach their most expensive years of higher education and training for jobs.

I do not believe these objections are substantial. Probably it is better that a woman in her menopause should be faced with a toddler who is tiring but uncomplicated rather than with an emotional teenage girl. Anyway, the objection presupposes that all women have a difficult menopause and this is not the case. Again, while the gulf between the generations is widening I do not think ten or fifteen years makes any crucial difference. This is essentially a matter of parents keeping communication with their children. Older parents can be more tolerant, more patient, and have broader sympathies and interests than younger couples; and parents of any age can be self-engrossed to an extent which makes them neglectful of their children. Fathers who retire when their children are teenagers have more time even if they have less money, and there are today many educational and training opportunities which young people can win for themselves. As for children preferring younger parents I do not think this is true either. Children with few exceptions love their parents, *good or bad, young or old*. They might become anxious if they thought their parents were so old as to be close to death; but health and expectation of life have been greatly improved.

Older parents wishing to adopt meet difficulties, and so, it appears, do most applicants who are not a hundred per cent healthy and conforming. The would-be parent who represents a 'harder case' is rarely given a chance. Refusal is automatic and references are not taken up.

'I have been a diabetic for nearly 14 years so know the ropes pretty well by now, and if a consultant from one of Britain's top teaching hospitals considers me fit and able to stand as an adoptive parent, I reckon I must be. But to try and convince the adoption

societies of this is another matter. They do not even wish to take up medical references.'

Home Counties housewife

This couple have a slightly retarded young daughter of their own and the girl seems to represent another insuperable barrier in the eyes of adoption officials.

'We would not have tried to adopt a baby in the first place had we not had the support of my specialist and our daughter's behind us . . .

The courage of this woman made no impression upon the many adoption agencies she approached. No one asked to see her. No references she supplied were taken up. My own feelings are that the timidity of the adoption workers in this case has denied some child a remarkable mother, who has faced with fortitude personal problems and so relegated them to sensible proportions that she has love enough left to embrace a homeless child. Sick of heart at her failure to persuade the agencies even to consider her case, she continues the search through third-party channels: such is the perseverance of love.

It appears as if adoption agencies are imprisoned within the unimaginative bounds of their well-meant naïvety. Their application of a mystically average couple as a yardstick is sometimes carried to the most bizarre lengths. One society even prefers their adopters to be of medium height.

'I was told of course if you are rather too short or rather too tall . . . it does take longer.'

Home Counties housewife

The most acceptable adopters are young (but not too young), middle-class, conventional in outlook and behaviour, and of average income from a safe job. Adopters must also appear to be 'settled'.

'We would give no guarantee that we should settle in this country and adoption societies apparently do not favour those who move about or go abroad.'

East Anglian housewife

Surely a child's security is largely with his loving parents, whether in an English village, New York or Timbuctoo! Adopters should not feel constrained to put down roots in this way. They are entitled to the same freedom to run their lives as natural parents enjoy, otherwise the children may suffer from the frustrations imposed upon their adoptive parents.

Sensing perhaps their own inadequacies, many adoption agencies are suspicious of the professional classes, particularly of those people who are qualified in their own or allied disciplines.

'I remarked it would be ironical if she did not think us suitable applicants in view of the fact I had worked as a child care officer. She smiled and replied that the department had recently turned down an application to adopt from a psychologist. The reason? He had done all the interviewing.'

Rejected former child care officer

'I knew—I felt—a lot about deprived children, adoption, emotional disturbance, social maladjustment, . . . The whole method of selection, the entire approach to the situation seems to me to be tragically at fault. But I am prejudiced. My ten years' experience with the pathetically inadequate social misfits of 14, 15, 16, my sympathy and understanding of the deprived, my horror at the criminal waste of human potential—all too often the result of a maladjusted home—all adds to my desire to see something done about adoption agencies.

I am not bitter, I am not resentful any more but I remain appalled at the inadequacy of the social agencies to solve some of the human problems of our day.'

Rejected teacher

It is ironical that those who have by their training special understanding of children should be treated with such distrust that their experience is counted against them and too often wasted. The transition is made from irony to tragic farce when one considers the part that religion plays in the selection of adoptive parents. There are societies with religious foundations and commitments; agencies exercising a more benevolent non-denominational selection; and local authorities officially without religious bias but often hamstrung by the stipulations of unmarried mothers or the religious proclivities of committee members. Religious conviction which should be a source of burning concern for deprived children of all races and creeds is the insurmountable barrier for many adopters of no formal religion or an unacceptable one.

'*We were rejected—probably because I was honest about my religious beliefs. I am a believer in a moral code based upon Christianity. I do not accept that Christ (if he existed) was the Son of God (if he exists). I do not go to Church. I do not believe in the After Life. But I do strongly believe that every human being should seek always to give happiness to others, to relieve pain and hurt and suffering, to show love to his fellows.*'

Teacher

'*We were visited several times by a representative of the adoption society. My wife and I had a medical examination and everything was satisfactory, but then came the request for a testimonial from the local vicar (others had been supplied from prestige people who knew us well) and this I declined to obtain. The vicar was my neighbour and I had no opinion of him and I am not a regular churchman. This I know to be a common enough picture. However I think a child was deprived of a good home.*'

Engineer

'*I pointed out that one could qualify by clocking in the requisite number of church attendances (some friends of ours did in fact do so). I then said this was a way of producing hypocrites, not Christians.*'

North Countryman

L

Most agnostics are firm in their disbelief and refuse to conceal it or renounce it. A few take the view that the ends justify the means.

'Although we have succeeded in adopting four children I know quite a lot about the difficulties involved. The biggest and most ridiculous obstacle that has to be overcome is the one of religion. We desperately wanted children and simply had to lie about this and pretend that we were regular churchgoers when we are in fact, agnostics. There must be many potential adopters who are prevented from taking children simply because they can't prove that they attend church.'

Postman's wife

It appears foolish for agnostics to apply to voluntary societies with church affiliations and religious stipulations, but the voluntary societies have familiar and evocative names. Dr. Barnardo's, for example, conjures up pictures of deprivation and homelessness and those in search of a child turn to them more readily than to the local Council. The voluntary societies still arrange more than three times as many adoptions as those local authorities which engage in the work as comparative newcomers. The well-known charities are rightly believed to have the most children to offer.

Local authorities are not bound to make any religious requirements of adopters. The officers arranging adoptions can be agnostics themselves, and sometimes, if the child is hard to place, will refer back to the mother and ask if she would be prepared to waive her wishes about religion in order that the child can be placed with an agnostic couple rather than lose the chance of adoption. This shows the right initiative.[3] Some unmarried mothers mistakenly regard the religious clause as a mere formality rather like murmuring 'C of E' upon admission to hospital.

The position for Jewish adopters is extraordinarily difficult. There are popular misconceptions that *all* Jews are orthodox, bound by the rigid prohibitions which spring from regarding Judaism as a race as well as a religion. In fact, Progressive Jews look upon Judaism simply as a religion and many of Britain's

450,000 Jews adopt this more liberal view. Orthodox Jews will only consider adopting a child who is fully Jewish by origin, with a Jewish mother and grandmother. A child in Progressive Judaism is regarded as Jewish if adopted by a Jewish couple and brought up as Jewish with Confirmation at sixteen. So adoption in a Progressive household is no intellectual or religious problem, but Jewish children are hardly ever available for adoption[4] and public attitudes towards Jews makes the likelihood of getting a Gentile child remote.

> '*We have been married thirteen years and have no children of our own. My husband is a consultant orthopaedic surgeon and I am a schoolteacher. For the past four years we have approached innumerable adoption societies and have now merely acquired a very large and very saddening file of refusals. None of these refusals states the reasons for rejection; we are well aware of them ourselves none the less. We are Jewish and therefore are turned down automatically by several societies. We contacted other societies without religious backing also unsuccessfully.*'
>
> Teacher

> '*Apart from the rejection by one Borough Child Care Officer, some other boroughs and voluntary organizations are not able even to consider us; we are middle-aged and Jewish (non-Orthodox).*'
>
> Social Worker

Both Agnostics and Jews are among those the Agnostics Adoption Agency seeks to help. This agency, established in 1963–4 with worth-while purposes and urgent needs to fulfil, unfortunately still has only one caseworker and is quite unable to meet the pressing demands on its services. Much of the criticism about the Christian bias of long-established adoption societies comes from Humanists, and if these influential Agnostics were moved to support their own adoption project more vigorously this agency would be finding homes each year for hundreds of children instead of fewer than a dozen. Nevertheless, it is heart-warming to find many Agnostics are idealists who wish to continue or complete their families with adopted children.

> '*I think the time will come in the quite near future when it is common practice for couples who have one or two children of their own and wish to have more to adopt unwanted children to augment their families.*'

Londoners

There are varying views about mixed families of natural and adopted children. Often the official attitude is cautious lest an adopted child might suffer feelings of inferiority if a natural child is born later. Or fears that the natural child might be favoured and seen to be preferred. This to my mind underestimates the qualities of adopters.

> '*Conscious of the problem of over-population in the world we felt we had amply reproduced ourselves . . . Our children are very precious to us. We have had a good marriage and family life and on top of this, my husband at 34 as an airline captain earns £4,000 a year . . . We are concerned about people who get such a raw deal from life when we are so fortunate ourselves.*'
>
> '*In our own case we did not apply to adopt because we think we are lovely people and someone ought to be glad to live with us. We would be delighted if the government and the powers-that-be would spend more money, time and effort in keeping families together. In the meantime we feel we have a lot to share and that some child could join the three already here in a secure happy home in a pleasant town with good available schools. We are aware of the special emotional problems of identification the adopted child may have, particularly in adolescence but we feel we could help him through these difficulties if they arose. However, XYZ Children's Department evidently think we are deluding ourselves.*'

Former child care officer

> '*My wife, 29, and I, 41, have three healthy sons, 6½, 4, and 15*

months. There are no little girls on either side of the family, and we have seriously considered adopting a girl to complete our family. We have decided this partly because the likelihood of a girl being born is substantially less than 50% and also because the world population explosion should discourage any further addition.

'*We approached our local council and were told the Adoption Committee would only consider parents who could produce a medical certificate to show that the birth of their own children was unlikely or medically undesirable. We cannot do this, and there the matter rests.*'

Doctor

'*We are becoming increasingly depressed and dejected that our offers of help are turned down, in spite of the apparent need for homes for these children.*'

Mother of six

These parents want an adopted child quite clearly for his own sake and as a social duty, not because they haven't any children or cannot have any more. However, such enthusiasm is suspect, and the more so if the couple offers a home to a coloured child.

'*We were asked if we knew any coloured people personally. The adoption officer said they preferred to place coloured children in families where they will have the chance of making friends with other coloured children, although the example she quoted of a Chinese baby recently placed in the family of a University Professor of Chinese did not seem wholly relevant! We told her that our neighbourhood is very mixed racially and the fact that we had no coloured people as close personal friends was simply the result of not having met any except casually.*

'*It is one of the characteristics of city life that one's friends are scattered; we have not even many intimate white friends in our immediate neighbourhood. It seems to be racial discrimination of another, but almost as misguided a kind, to feel one must make friends among West Indian or African families* only *because of their colour. We tried to make this clear to the adoption officer, but had the uneasy impression she felt we were probably rather unsociable people anyway.'*

Teacher's wife

'*I am a socialist and an atheist and wish to help in every possible way towards alleviating the suffering or neglect of the majority of the inhabitants of the world.*

'*I feel strongly that in this country adopting a coloured or half-coloured baby is one of the means open to me. My husband feels the same way. We are both fond of children and want to see them live full and satisfying lives with every chance to develop.'*

London housewife

'*We have now two children, and, of course, wouldn't wish it otherwise. I long to have more but feel even more guilty now that we should be doing more than simply replacing ourselves. We should particularly like a Chinese, Vietnamese or similar baby.'*

East Coast housewife

'*It is a sad reflection that we had to resort to a private arrangement with another country to get a child because of the authorities in England and their inflexible laws.'*

Adoptive mother of a Turkish child

'*We simply wanted a baby girl of any race or of mixed race . . . Somebody finally took a faint interest. We went through all the usual lengthy business and then were nearly turned down when they discovered that our eight year old daughter had convulsive fits. They wouldn't like* one of their babies *to see a child in a fit. I managed to convince them that it was a very long time since she had had one and was not likely to have another. Eventually we were offered a baby. She is now a lovely happy little girl and I often think how near she came to growing up in an institution.'*

Postman's wife

'We had a young baby and wished to adopt a child who might not otherwise have a home. We told the adoption society we might decide later to have another child of our own but this would, of course, make no difference to our love and care of our adopted child. We had thought about the possibility of adopting a coloured baby for four years but in a letter of rejection we were told the Committee felt that you should not rush into the adoption of a coloured child and that you ought to be absolutely sure that in not having more natural children you are not denying your daughter and yourselves something very precious.'

London housewife

Strange words indeed from adoption officials to whom adopted children and natural children ought to be regarded as equally 'precious'. Why is there this official determination to keep love and coloured children at arm's length? The adoptions officer of one London borough explained her view to me in these words: 'These couples want a coloured child for intellectual reasons. *They feel guilt about the colour question and they are hoping in this way to solve the colour problem. Theirs is often a sudden impulse and better parents are those who will take any child and will not insist he is coloured.'* Such attitudes defeat the warm generosity of the world. Adoption workers may protest that coloured children are wanted for adoption as proof of the parents' altruism, justification of their agnosticism, or as a gesture against apartheid; but the children are *wanted*. The doctrinaire adoption officer insists the coloured child must be wanted only *for himself*. Such a dogma ignores the complex, if not unconscious, nature of people's motives. These are seldom simple or completely unselfish.

All those who wrote to me who wished to adopt coloured children were Agnostics or Jews. Yet the International Social Service which brings coloured babies to Britain for adoption[5] has made two denominational societies (Barnardo's and the National Children's Home) legal guardians for the children and responsible for screening the adopters. This means that these children can go only into Christian homes, so the hopes of would-be Agnostics and Jewish adopters are dashed again. In my view the I.S.S. betrays its constitution by this move because it professes to be 'a private international organization without national, political, racial, or religious bias'.

Prospective parents of coloured children certainly persevere in their attempts to find official approval. Their letters have a genuine fire, and despair within them. It is impossible to recount in detail all their experiences, but one example will illustrate the frustrations of many who seek to adopt a coloured child.

Here is the diary of London housewife, MARY, married with two daughters:

MARCH: Went to local children's department, got list of adoption societies including LCC which did not impose religious obligations.

    Wrote to these three sources.

    One replied they would not consider couples with children. One would not consider us unless we were Catholic or coloured. Wrote back we should be delighted to adopt a coloured child even though we were not coloured ourselves. Had long correspondence with the secretary, culminating in an interview with the chairman. Welcoming although suspicious of our attitude and worried about our 2 bed-roomed flat. Visited us at home and realized we genuinely intended to move to a bigger flat when we had another child.

OCT: Wrote accepting our offer. Would we consider a West Indian girl about five months. Thanked them, repeated we should like a baby from earliest possible age but if that was not possible would certainly consider older baby.

NOV: Another letter saying Society had now decided not to place any more coloured children—instead placing them with church adoption societies. Would understand if we wished to apply elsewhere.

    Reapplied to the LCC whom we had informed of our acceptance by the Society.

DEC: LCC will consider us if we foster one of their children in care for them to assess us.

JAN: Midwife from Ghana rang me. Would I foster her $2\frac{1}{2}$ months old baby? Yes, and LCC agreed to assess me on results.

Baby appeared nervous wreck, continually sick, severe eczema, terrified of everything.

Few days later mother told me she and the father had been fighting and rowing every night. She was beginning to fear for the baby. She came 3–4 times a week to see Jonathan and each time he became highly upset and screamed for hours. His father came once or twice; the baby almost had hysterics at the sight of him. Hard-going, but Jonathan was a highly responsive, charming, happy and affectionate baby alongside his nervousness and he loved our children and they adored him. He more than made up for the hard work.

AUG: Jonathan left us. He was much calmer and obviously not frightened any more. LCC welfare officer came twice, said she was delighted with us and thought we would make ideal adoptive parents. But repeated constantly *it was not up to her*.

SEPT: Filled in a form formally requesting a child for adoption. Made no stipulation about age or sex. But the adoption agency was transferred from the LCC to the local borough authority.

DEC: Rang local council asking why the delay.
Received a letter *thanking us for our offer of adoption but regretting they could not accept it*.

JAN: Heard of possible baby through third party.

FEB: Rang third party who told me mother had decided to keep the baby.

MARCH: TWO years since we applied to adopt. Gave up.

NOV: Our third child was born. Shall probably have another baby of our own soon. Don't think either of us will ever again want to face the immediate deep official suspicion we got in almost every case except from the third party.

Barnardo's in 1967 were getting a letter every day asking them to take a coloured child for adoption. All agencies are short of parents for children of mixed races and yet the problem remains comfortably removed from public awareness. No Home Secretary has ever appeared on television to appeal for thousands of homes for coloured babies. One might be on the screen tomorrow urging respect for law and order when the unloved tearaways from a generation of children, white and coloured, bring forth the harvest of the deprived.

Meanwhile, there is no urgency in the present climate of adoption.

> *'The adoptions officer had to go on leave of absence for some time, consequently all adoptions were to be held in abeyance for several months.'*

London housewife

NOTES

1. There is a shortage of Roman Catholic adopters.
2. See p. 123.
3. It is to be noted that the consent form for High Court adoptions does not include any reference to the religious persuasion in which the child is to be brought up.
4. Jewish family bonds are so close that only rarely is a baby given for adoption. There is no Jewish Adoption Society because of this scarcity of Jewish babies.
5. Its Hong Kong project was inaugurated in 1960, to find homes for Chinese babies, World Refugee Year.

11

New Developments

ONE hundred years ago a 'Beadle' employed by Dr. Barnardo was charged 'to raise the fallen, to cheer the faint and to infuse fresh courage into the discouraged warriors in the grim battle of life'. Old ideas reappear in modern dress and the Children and Young Persons Act of 1963 does not use such sanctimonious language but it gives much the same brief to local authority children's officers. Moreover, Barnardo's 'Deaconesses' were upper-class counterparts of today's 'home helps', except that they were not so fastidious about what they did. In houses where the mother was sick, they cleaned, cooked, minded the children; and they were social workers too.

The Deaconesses befriended families threatened with eviction and often stood between them and their landlords. Always, they strove to keep families together. They provided food and clothes, lent sewing-machines, mangles, tools of employment, and arranged holidays for the overworked. The same role is defined for the local authorities in the 1963 Act which explicitly tells them to do all they can to prevent family separations and to lessen the need to take children into care or before the courts. They have a remarkably free hand to help in kind or with cash, but there is an equally remarkable reticence about the ways in which these powers are employed.

The Home Office report on the work of local children's departments between the three years 1964 and 1966[1] is not an inspiring record of initiative and imagination. The section devoted to new ideas for prevention and rehabilitation occupies less than a page. It also provides the official excuse for lack of enterprise: 'The provision of support for the family, designed to promote the

171

welfare of the children and to diminish the need to receive them into care, is still in the early stage of development. . . . Much remains to be done, but an encouraging start has been made . . .' This reassurance is the harder to accept when one discovers that in spite of the new powers and the efforts of nearly a thousand more child care workers,[2] the numbers of children in local authority care at the end of March 1966 was the highest recorded, 69,157.[3]

The Home Office points out, of course, that there are many more children in the country. The 1966 total of children in care represents 5·3 per thousand of the estimated population under eighteen: in parentage terms only slightly more than the 1959 figure of 5·1 per thousand. This sounds reasonable enough. It is tempting to take pride in 'negative achievement', but the extent of the positive disaster is not reflected in national percentages. It is revealed within the separate classifications of child need. Here, if the 1962–3 Home Office report is used as a yardstick, the latest figures show that the number of children admitted into care because of unsatisfactory homes was up 81 per cent in 1966. By that time too the number of abandoned or lost children needing official care had increased by 50 per cent. There was also a 38 per cent rise in the total of illegitimate children whose mothers felt obliged to hand them over to the local authorities, and the number of cases in which a family was deserted by the mother and the father was unable to manage increased by 31 per cent.

Nothing in the report testifies to effective preventive measures inspired by the 1963 Act. Everything confirms the depressing and massive area of need for swift remedies.

It might be argued that it is premature to look for dramatic results. Perhaps the strength of new schemes lies in the forethought gone into their foundation and improvements will be marked in the next triennial report[4] of the Home Office. One can only hope so. Meanwhile, the casualties of slow-moving reforms are young children whose needs are immediate and pressing.

To find out more for myself I wrote at random (September 1967) to nine local authorities asking for the reports covering the work of the children's departments. Only one authority

(LEICESTER) sent me an up-to-date publication covering the period April 1965 to March 1967. The last published report on the work of the BIRMINGHAM children's department was fourteen years out of date. It covered the period 1949–53. A report on the last three years was being printed but, presumably, Birmingham's work with children in need in the ten years between the two reports is to be unrecorded.

The children's officer for the London borough of CAMDEN sent me detailed reports on the development of preventive work up to the end of March 1966 and a memorandum prepared by the children's committee about the exercise of parental rights to the detriment of foster-children.[5]

DEVON children's department do not publish annual reports and their last publication spanned twenty years (1944–64). 'We have no spare copies now and, of course, it is out of date.'

GLOUCESTERSHIRE'S children's officer wrote that her annual report is for the information of members of the Gloucestershire Children's Committee. What use would I make of the report if I were allowed to see it? Was I receiving any backing for my book from the child care associations?

I was told by LEEDS children's officer that the annual report for the year ending March 1967 had not been published. No copies were left of the previous year's report but I did get one for the year ending March 1965. 'This report contains the general principles applying to the department, and the major changes would be in relation to statistics.'

LIVERPOOL produces no annual report but if I would indicate any specific information the children's officer 'would look into the matter of supplying it'.

The last published report of the SOMERSET'S children's officer dealt with 1961–3 and there was no news of a later one. WILTSHIRE'S latest report was two to three years out of date when I wrote and an annual report is not published.

It is a surprisingly lax state of affairs that reports are not produced and widely distributed *every year* by *all* children's departments. If current developments in children's work cannot be studied freely, opportunities for constructive research are lost and exchange of ideas and experience made the more difficult. More important, the citizen is kept in ignorance and private consciences are undisturbed.

Children's departments may be short-staffed and under-financed, but they cannot afford to neglect businesslike procedures.

The percentage of children boarded out by local authorities is on record but there are no figures showing how many of these foster arrangements fail. Unhappy children, like misaddressed parcels, are moved around in search of acceptance and the more relevant statistics concern these failures.

Similarly with adoption, it is important to keep records of those who are not helped (both mothers wanting babies adopted and would-be adopters) and the reasons why. How many children are re-adopted? Facts are needed to supplant fallacies and to create an informed and strong body of opinion to initiate and influence modern developments.

I studied four months' copies of the weekly *Municipal Journal* without finding any reports or opinions or new ideas in children's work. Only a few facts from the Home Office report on work between 1964 and 1966 received attention in a news item.

Voluntary societies are more aware of the need for informing the public. The reasons for this are obvious. They need to raise money and are well aware of the handicap of appearing old-fashioned as well as old-established. As a result their publications are comparatively voluminous and informative. They are also compelled by law to produce yearly reports and accounts. Nearly all of the voluntary agencies belong to the Standing Conference of Societies Registered for Adoption, an organization devoted to self-improvement. Unfortunately, under its present constitution local authorities cannot join, so although the Standing Conference is the only body in this country representing adoption agencies the eighty or more local councils engaged in the work are excluded. The absurdity of the situation, which must owe much to mutual jealousies and suspicions, is at last being recognized. There is refreshing talk of restyling the organization to meet modern needs.

The Standing Conference holds adoption conferences and has a variety of publications including a quarterly journal.[6] It also runs training courses under its recently appointed tutor, Miss Jane Rowe, and for the first time has staff and resources for research. The Conference now co-operates with the Home Office, giving information from members about the operation of adoption law and ideas for improvement. An editorial in *Child Adoption* (No. 52) 1967 is ingenuously honest: 'The need for more information has long been felt and for some years many of us have realized that we did not know even the basic facts about adoption practice or whether even our most firmly cherished working principles had any basis in reality. The challenge to acquire more information therefore comes not just from a government department but from our own uneasiness about the state of affairs.'

Developments reviewed in this chapter are recorded in the meagre Home Office literature, reports from children's officers, specialist journals;[7] publications of the National Council for the Unmarried Mother and Her Child; newspaper cuttings and personal interviews. If there are important omissions, I only hope this book will stimulate the speedy publication of such enterprise elsewhere.

In this country with its legion of misplaced loyalties to the past, the most important development in adoption work lies not in new ideas but in multiplication of effort, notably from the many more local councils now choosing to arrange adoptions.

The growing involvement of local authorities with adoption shows a new and responsible awareness of the worsening size of the problem, and means more money and minds are being invested in solutions. Most satisfactory of all, their wider participation opens up more agencies uncommitted to a narrow religious base of operations. Most local authorities claim to be emancipated from inflexible rules about religion, ages, health.

One would like to seize upon this change of attitude with unalloyed pleasure; but one set of arbitrary standards is often replaced by another. The equally restricting and pretentious game of 'depth interviewing' practised by the adoption workers of some councils denies and bewilders many would-be adopters as frustratingly as some voluntary society's rules. And this although adoption caseworkers are not psychiatrists. Untutored to observe psychiatric factors it seems unlikely they will learn a great deal more after half a dozen interviews than after one or two. This local authority approach to adoption often digs its own pitfalls and these fashionable psychological charades produce too many undeserving casualties.

More genuine liberalism and frontiersmanship is often inspired by the enthusiasm of voluntary organizations: but it is one thing to identify needs and another to meet them adequately. The Agnostics Adoption Society produces a good example of the problem. It was founded to serve the increasing number of potential adopters who do not conform to the requirements of most agencies. The sponsors believe that local authorities who should arrange adoptions on a secular basis often leave the work to the voluntary societies, or appoint a supervising committee which has views similar to those of the religious societies.

Their own enterprise seeks to help agnostics, non-Church-going Christians, couples of mixed religion, Jews, and those who have been involved in divorces. They offer a full casework service to unmarried mothers and this includes short-term fostering of babies from hospital. This society is 'flooded with applications' and has only one caseworker.

In the first six months of its active life 144 pairs of prospective adopters were interviewed but only twenty-six approved. The high rejection figure was attributed to applications from other societies' rejects. 'Initially many couples applied to us who had already been refused by several societies on grounds other than religion, hoping that our general standards might be lower.' This unhappily suggests that the Agnostics Society might also be bedevilled by those inhibiting and unadventurous concepts which stand in the way of placing all possible children and suiting all possible parents. In five years the society's work continues to make slow progress and its original plan to expand across the country remains as yet a pipe-dream.

Another good idea, if limited, led in 1965 to the British Adoption Project—an investigation into the problems of adopting non-European babies in Britain. The joint sponsors are International Social Service and London University. The project has the backing of the Home Office and is being financed by charitable trusts and local authorities. The research will last four years and during this time fifty babies under one year, of half or full Asian, African or West Indian parentage will be found adoptive homes in London and the Home Counties. Each adoption will be closely observed, with the adoptive parents as willing partners in the research. The project aims to demonstrate that coloured babies can be placed successfully and to reveal the best methods of recruiting and selecting adopters.

The difficulty is that no one knows how many coloured children in Britain need adoptive families. The project itself receives an average of fifteen requests a month from the London area alone, but most agencies have no figures of the number of coloured babies who are not even offered for adoption. A permanent adoption resource exchange for coloured children is wanted and the project's plans for this were well under way at the end of 1967. The exchange will help agencies place those children they cannot find homes for, and make sure that suitable adopters are not wasted because they happen to live in an area where few or no coloured children are needing parents. The exchange could also serve as a central clearing house for inquiries about adopting a coloured child.

This idea of a resource exchange makes excellent sense and should be widely introduced to help all homeless and parentless children. For adoptions to be stymied by the territorial limits of various agencies is bureaucratic nonsense, stark administrative madness when the happiness of a child is at stake.

Vigorous efforts to meet the challenge of children difficult to place are made by the Crusade of Rescue, a Catholic Child Care Society which handles over a thousand cases every year. In 1963 they started to keep an official list of harder cases. It was found that children who were having to wait more than six months for homes were often coloured or of mixed ancestry. Other problem children had physical or mental handicaps. Some were over two

M

years old and showing disturbed behaviour. There were also children of poor or doubtful background.

All child care officers had copies of the list which was reviewed at fortnightly meetings attended by all field workers. Many means were explored to find homes for these children. Newspaper advertisements produced only small and mostly unrealistic response. Talks were more effective and best results came when child care officers could be present to lead informal discussion groups. Co-operation with Catholic child care societies in other parts of the country was profitably stepped up; exceptional needs were made widely known and up-to-date information was given to all who might be able to help. Alongside these more energetic efforts to improve the placement prospects of children on the list, more time was made to work with any mother who plans to provide for her child.

Work with unmarried mothers and their babies is the special contribution of the Coram Foundation for Children, one of the oldest children's charities and yet one of the most forward looking. They find foster-homes for illegitimate babies to give mothers time to plan, and 60 per cent of these babies are returned to their natural mothers within two years. [8]

There is virtually no breakdown in the fostering arrangements, for foster-parents are left in no doubt that only serious illness or death justifies the child's return to anyone but the mother. The society helps about eighty mothers every year and at any one time has some 350 babies in foster-homes. They will only help a mother once.

Many very young mothers go to them and so do a large number of students. The Foundation runs its own residential nursery where babies spend an average time of six to eight weeks, before going to a carefully selected foster-home. Mothers keep in close touch and everything is done to make sure they reach a realistic decision within a reasonable time.

Coram feel the work they are doing could be extended if they had greater means. I was told: 'We are doing work not done by anybody else and when we see the happiness of a young couple who get married and can have their own child back, even this two years wait has been well worth while, not only for the baby but for the parents.'

Many believe, however, that Coram's successes are hand-picked and most mothers and their babies need to grow together in close physical contact, or they will grow away from one another. There is certainly psychiatric evidence of damage if a child of one or two has to change mothers.

Hospitality within private families for pregnant unmarried girls both before and after the baby is born would be an improvement on Coram's scheme. This provides time for a decision to be made and also allows the mother opportunity to get to know her baby and what is involved in looking after him. Some psychiatrists see the mother's own care of the baby as a 'tender trap', but it is also a test of the practical realities and restrictions involved in baby care. Of course, finding suitable private hospitality is difficult. The hostess to an unmarried mother should never give advice. Mistrust of the unmarried mother as a temptress or as a person 'bad for the children' will destroy the arrangement. Such prejudices exist but the National Council for the Unmarried Mother and Her Child receives ten to twelve offers a week of accommodation for pregnant girls. They now have 600 addresses of facilities offering accommodation. Unfortunately, perhaps, half of these families are wanting domestic services in return, and few of those who write to the Council offer to take in any unmarried mother and her baby.

There is both good heart and sound sense in keeping unmarried mothers and their children in the community, especially the pathetic girls who are but children themselves and older women who set a premium on privacy and independence. Too few doors are open to them.

For inadequate young mothers not mature enough to be left to look after their babies unaided there are a few hostels open as 'half-way houses'. One in Monmouthshire caters for half a dozen mothers who can stay with their babies for at least a year attending classes under the guidance of a 'house mother'. During the day a nurse minds the babies while the girls go out to work. This hostel is run by the County Council, but Barnardo's too are experimenting with short-stay homes and hostels for unmarried mothers with their babies.[9]

For the more socially self-sufficient unmarried mothers housing schemes operate in a few places. No doubt these help one group of unmarried mothers, but it is difficult to assess the true extent of the need for these projects. They are mostly voluntary welfare enterprises of local inspiration and nothing has been done to find out what extension of the idea might be worth while.

A new trend is to provide accommodation for fatherless families alongside that for unmarried mothers, in attempts to avoid feelings of social ostracism. Housing Trusts are playing an increasingly important role. The Haverstock Housing Trust, London, buys houses to run on a non-profit making basis as flatlets for unsupported mothers—half of the tenants will be widowed, divorced, or separated, and half unmarried. The flatlets are small so the families accepted must be limited to one or two children. There are no communal services except a laundry, and day care of children must be arranged with nurseries and baby-minders. I understand there is no wish to run this as a permanent charity and rents will not be subsidized except in emergencies. The idea is that the flats will provide a permanent home and no one will ever be asked to leave except under the most exceptional circumstances.

A particularly enlightened and thoughtful enterprise is Family First, Nottingham, which is a housing association and a charity. Its objectives are to build homes or find them (often by convincing landlords that unsupported mothers can be good tenants) and to provide any necessary service not forthcoming from an existing agency. The first housing project gives eight expectant mothers well-equipped bed-sitting rooms with kitchen recesses. They can stay for up to five months before the baby's birth and as long as necessary afterwards. There is no paid warden, but a three-generation family living as tenants help to create a more natural atmosphere. The second stage of the scheme envisages building sixteen self-contained flats on the site for unsupported mothers with children. A day nursery is also planned and will be available for some non-resident children.

Other homes offering bed-sitters to unmarried mothers impose a tenancy limit of two years or less, and have more rules. One run by the Birmingham Diocesan Council for Family and Social Welfare locks its front door at 11.0 p.m. It also appears that the tenancies can be terminated by one week's notice. Another project, in Exmouth, also run by the Diocesan Council, opened in December 1963 without a resident supervisor. Complaints about tenants' behaviour were made to the Town Council and 'because there was nobody to confirm the girls' side of the story' the house was closed. After a time it was re-opened with a mature student-teacher living in 'to help maintain respectability'.

At a home I visited in North London, run by the West London Mission, all the girls had their own front door keys and were completely independent. All went out to work leaving their babies in the day nursery on the premises. Eight out of twenty-one girls married within two years (only one to the baby's father) and most of them left better qualified to earn more money because they were inspired by the warden and the energy of other mothers to attend evening classes.

How difficult is it for an unmarried working mother to arrange good day care for her baby? Since 1948 the number of local authority day nurseries has been halved, but there are more than eight times the number of private nurseries,[10] and a number of charitable societies are now caring for the children of unmarried mothers on a daily or weekly basis.

It is perhaps not widely known that the Ministry of Social Security is willing to help an unmarried girl with a part-time job by paying the cost of day care for her baby. In fact, improved supplementary allowances are such that unless a girl has a highly paid job she is as well off drawing them. She can then afford to stay at home with her baby; or to take an undemanding part-time job at which she can earn £2 a week without loss of benefit. Most mothers who keep their babies prefer to make sacrifices and go to work all day. To accept a fixed income permitting only a simple living is not an inviting prospect when young. It needs maturity to pension yourself off to look after a baby.

NOTES

1. Home Office Report on the Work of the Children's Department, 1964–6 (H.M.S.O. 603, 1967).

2. The field staff (staff primarily engaged in work with individual children and their families) went up from 1,549 in March 1963 to 2,341 in March 1966 —an increase of 51 per cent.

3. The 1967 total of children in the care of local authorities and voluntary organizations taken together (79,268) shows a slight decline for the first time since 1959. Children in the care of local authorities rose only to 69,405.

4. A Home Office paper is published annually giving bare statistics about children in care. Fuller information is given in the Reports on the Work of the Home Office Children's Department which now appear triennially. Previous reports were less frequent; there was a gap of six years between publications in 1955 and 1961.

5. Copies of this have been sent to the Home Secretary, the Association of Municipal Corporations, the London Boroughs Association, and local M.P.s.

6. *Child Adoption*, a lively and widely informative publication edited by Margaret Kornitzer.

7. *Child Adoption*, the Journal of the Standing Conference of Societies Registered for Adoption; and *Child Care News*, published by the Association of Child Care Officers.

8. About 15 per cent are adopted and 25 per cent left in foster-care.

9. In 1968 Lancashire County Council opened a special unit where pregnant girls sent to approved schools will be able to keep their babies. It is the first in Britain.

10. Since 1948 the number of council nurseries has been cut from 910 looking after 43,000 children to 448 in 1965 looking after 21,000 children. Private nurseries have increased from 250 with 7,000 children to 2,200 with 55,000 children. (Miss Joan Lester reporting in the House of Commons on 25 April 1967.)

12

Conclusions

THE numbers of illegitimate children continue to rise, and radical reforms are needed to see these children do not pay appalling penalties for their parents' permissiveness. There is no humanity in savage condemnation, but good purpose in making clear the responsibilities which go with sexual licence when this so often leads to a child without love, not to a love-child.

A great deal can be done to impress upon boys, generally more promiscuous than girls, that they have the larger initiative and responsibility in intelligent enjoyment of sex. Boys are often older than their partners and the instigators, if not the seducers. It is they who should be indoctrinated with the idea that to use contraceptives is sophisticated in the best sense of the word.

Psychiatrists suggest that many unmarried mothers need a baby as a love-object to compensate for lack of love in their own lives. Normal boys do not need a baby: their drive stems from burgeoning manhood, and manliness should mean the maturity to enjoy sex without unnecessary fears of an unwanted baby. Sex education for boys is widely neglected by schools and parents. Boys have imaginations as well as sex organs and they should be helped to realize the desolation of a mother parting with her baby, the barrenness of institutions and the stark tragedy of babies without parents.

Such tuition needs underpinning with effective social sanctions against those who father bastards. The first of these is the identification of as many such fathers as possible. Courts should have the power to order blood tests in affiliation cases. Drivers suspected of excessive drinking must now undergo blood tests at the request of the police. It is as important to identify a child's parentage as to prove a motorist drunk: the child has the prior right, to know his own father. I am not recommending shot-gun weddings, but unmarried fathers should be named and made to contribute fairly towards the child's upkeep. It is a typical English compromise that sneaking admiration for the man 'who's a bit of a rake' means that failure to pay up under a Court affiliation order is subject to comparatively light penalties.

I suggest that any man who does not honour such legal debts to his child and the mother should be declared a bankrupt. Such a penalty should be a particularly effective deterrent to a young man. Until he met his debts he would not be able to engage in business on his own account, or secure a loan for mortgage or motor-cycle. Presumably, he would also be a man marked for special scrutiny by Inland Revenue; and, of course, his assets could be seized and realized to discharge his affiliation debts.

Only about 8 per cent of mothers of bastards are awarded the present maximum of fifty shillings a week and the percentage is bound to go down when the maximum is raised. The average award in 1966 was thirty-three shillings. Practical considerations dictate these figures, for some of these fathers are very young— some are married and supporting second families; and of the fathers before the Courts in 1965 an estimated 80 per cent were earning less than £14 a week. The point remains, however, that there should be no upper limit for an award under an affiliation order. Obviously a millionaire father can afford a great deal and all cases should be decided on the individual circumstances.

Continental courts adopt this practice and, moreover, it is realized that getting an order is one thing, getting the money another. In this country a quarter of affiliation payments fall into arrears within six months, half within the first year and three-quarters within two years. Week by week many British mothers do not know whether money under a court order is coming or not. They must hang around the court to find out, for most court collecting officers will not say on the telephone if the money is waiting or not. In Britain, as in many other countries, the State should underwrite these payments and recover from fathers in default by enforcing a range of new penalties such as bankruptcy for backsliders.

Unmarried parents have many rights, but the question of their personal responsibility is often shirked. Social conscience dictates that their unwanted babies must be cared for but it is not enough to delegate their care to the local authority or a children's home. All children need deeply rooted ties and the security of one or two parents who can provide the background for a fulfilling childhood. The parents' best atonement to the illegitimate child is an early and firm decision about his future. Now mothers can change their minds about adoption and the natural fathers may challenge the arrangement. The confusion of English law on this matter is such that a father's consent to his child's adoption is unnecessary: although, since the 1959 Illegitimacy Act, he may intervene by applying for custody himself. So adopters are on emotional tenterhooks until the signing of the order. If the claims of natural parents are preferred, the baby who has been in the care of prospective adopters has to transfer his love and trust. This cannot be achieved with a stroke of the pen. More reasonably, both natural mothers and fathers should be required to sign consent forms to adoption which are irrevocable.

Of course, they should not be under any pressure to sign. On the other hand why encourage the agony of indecision with so many legal hedges? In Ontario a mother may not give her consent until the child is a week old but only during the three weeks after signing can she revoke her consent. In Australia mothers cannot change their minds after thirty days from the date on which they signed their consent. These laws bear more kindly on all the parties concerned.

While I advocate stiffer penalties for unmarried fathers, I see no point in showing the unmarried mother anything other than loving kindness and practical help. This may sound invidious discrimination, but it must be clearly understood that the child's sound development depends on the equilibrium of his mother. If she feels rejected and insecure how is she to mother her baby satisfactorily? The baby's world is his mother and all his earliest impressions are coloured by her attitudes.

It is rightly said that unmarried mothers need outside stimulus and companionship. Otherwise, they may grow resentful and reject the baby or form an obsessively emotional attachment to the child. Too often the urge to get back 'to the office' experienced by many unmarried mothers is an indictment of an uncaring community. Basic social security allowances are reasonable and the Ministry, although loath to advertise such generosity, is prepared to meet reasonable rent and other commitments. Financially, an unmarried mother can often be just as well off at home with her baby as out to work in shop or office. To be at home contentedly, however, she needs the friendship and kindness of neighbours. Visits from social workers are no substitute. There are proposals for new laws to provide higher affiliation awards, tighter controls on child-minding, and increased protection for the inheritance rights of children adopted abroad by British citizens. Some of this legalistic tidying is useful, but it side-steps the real heart of the problem, the explosive question of parental rights. It is here that legal reform should start.

I believe there should be a maximum period for fostering of one year, and that parents should have to plead in court for further time in which to provide a home for their child, or release him for adoption. This may appear hard and uncompassionate. Opponents of the idea will not hesitate to say so and to condemn interference with parental rights and the alleged strength of the blood-tie as something sacrilegious.

Nevertheless, arguments in favour of such radical reform are more convincing. Proposals to take away rights from neglectful parents after three years are being considered by some M.P.s, local authorities, and agencies. In my view this is too long a period of licence. The evidence about deprivation in infancy shows conclusively that if a child is institutionalized for three years his personality and intelligence may suffer irreparable damage. Also if he is fostered for so long a period he will mourn his foster-mother if removed from the home. The fact is that the stark tragedy of a homeless child requires clear-cut solutions and there should be only two alternatives before the parents. They should either take the child home again or be compelled to offer him for adoption. To compromise is to squander the child's happiness.

Social agencies have been rightly criticized by child experts for accepting children on a 'temporary' basis without plans for the future. A decision is indefinitely postponed while the parents are relieved of immediate care. This is foolishness and at last officially recognized as such. Under the wide powers of the Children and Young Persons Act 1963 councils can spend all the time and money they can afford to keep children out of care and to assist families, however incomplete, to stay together.

The results so far appear to be negligible, but schemes to help motherless families, to educate and rehabilitate inadequate families, to guarantee rents to avoid evictions, and to support unmarried mothers all exist. State security allowances are enough for an unmarried mother and child to live on. I suspect that if local authorities were saved the vast amount of time and resources expended to find and supervise foster-homes, they could devote more vigour and imagination to this worth-while work.

My belief is that it should be possible to help a parent or parents to organize their children back into their lives within a year. If parents fail to do so they are useless in their roles as mother and father and their children should not be precluded from a real home.

Of course, there are exceptional cases of hardship when illnesses, accidents, or housing shortages defeat the best intentions. Such cases should get sympathy in the court and help from the welfare agencies. What has to be remembered, however, is that it is irrelevant to consider for too long whether parents are *unable* or *unwilling* to provide: the result is the same, a bereaved child.

The plan might be attacked on the grounds that older children from broken families with deep loyalties to natural parents would resent adoption into new families. They would reject a change of name as symbolically cutting links with their past, however unsatisfactory or sordid. Undoubtedly, the tie between parent and child is deep and although it can be greatly distorted, is not to be expunged by mere physical separation. Recognition of this is embodied within existing adoption law: an older child must agree to his adoption. The Guardian *ad litem* must be sure that the child, if of an age to understand what is happening, knows that he is being adopted, and approves.

If the older child did not feel able to accept his foster-parents as adopters, an attempt should be made to find him fresh adopters. Alternatively, if it was the idea of adoption he was against and not his foster-parents, they should be enabled to ask for legal custody so that he could grow up undisturbed in their care.

It is argued that because children brought up by substitute parents are curious about their natural parents, are often grieved by their initial rejection, and may have difficulties in realizing their own identities, the principle of adoption is not as good as it seems. It ignores the blood-tie.

So far as young children are concerned their love-bond is with the people who have cherished them, and it is the ties of infancy which are lasting. When older, they are bound to be curious about their origins. This is right and healthy. Their curiosity should be respected and not feared, for the blood-tie is largely a myth kept alive by popular romanticism. A girl from an approved school was shown on television meeting her mother after some fifteen years. She was impassive about it. 'I don't want to go back.' Another institution child wrote in adulthood: 'I didn't discover my mother until I was grown-up and married. I only asked out of curiosity. I went to visit her in an old people's home. She meant nothing to me.'

I suspect that much-loved adopted children suffer not so much from feelings of rejection and deep personal regrets as from fossilized public attitudes towards blood and lineage. The British particularly suffer from ancestor worship and reveal extraordinary snobbery about family tradition. The Latin tags on many a family coat of arms proclaim purity and virtue while the lineage records bastardy.

On the one hand there are lingering popular misconceptions and deep-seated prejudices. On the other, from many ill-trained professional workers a similar hostility based upon half-digested studies of psychiatry. Both are examples of a little knowledge being dangerous and in the sphere of adoption they combine to produce an atmosphere in which prospective adopters are made to feel that homeless children need to be safeguarded from their enthusiasm and love. The latest psychological barrier obstructing adopters is suspicion that their application to adopt may be a 'cry for help' for *themselves*. Such a wish conceals insufficient personalities, an unhealthy need for dependants, and many other tortuous psychic defects which loom in the imaginations of many under-trained social workers.

Local authorities and religious societies talk solicitously and possessively about 'our children' who must be protected. The truth is that councils and charities can feed and house children but cannot embrace them as parents. No child can love a house-mother as his own. She has to be shared among too many and will probably leave for a better job in a year or two. This pathetic destruction of the child's world is allowed to go on because ignorance and complacency go hand in hand, and the selection of foster-parents and would-be adopters allows for a self-satisfying fastidiousness.

'I just couldn't see her nursing a baby,' an adoptions officer said to me talking of a woman she had refused. The baby's contribution to the woman's maternalism was not anticipated. Many new mothers are awkward and clumsy with their infants; the baby loves them just the same if they communicate their love for him.

Adoption workers admit there are no established criteria for assessing adopters. Decisions are a subjective mixture of hunch and theory. There have been few follow-up studies and, although more extensive research is in progress, I have reservations about the worth of these studies. Much of the information will inevitably have to be obtained in interview with adopters and children and the honesty of answers to some of the more searching questions must be suspect. Again, research cannot rate the 'success' of an adoption because success has so many interpreta-tions. How and when is it to be judged? Probably the only sure register of failure is the number of re-adoptions and these figures are not recorded, or at any rate, not available to the public.

Adoption workers wear long faces when they speak of their

heavy responsibilities, and rightly emphasize that a 'bad' place-ment could cause a child grievous suffering. This is so, but the most unsuitable home may possibly be better than life as an emotional hermit in an institution or the child experiencing a succession of foster-homes.

In any event, the hard truth is that there are no gilt-edged adop-tees or adopters and life is full of risks which cannot be eliminated.

The biggest mistake made by the assessors probably lies in regarding adoption as a 'job' instead of a relationship. The most modern psychological tests, with computers to analyse the results, can no more gurantee 'safe' adoptions than marriage bureaux promise happy marriages. Anybody may fall ill, go mad, turn against their families, take to crime or drink. Bad parents can always cause children to suffer, although any N.S.P.C.C. inspector will vouch for the fact that these children still do not want to be parted from their parents.

It might be argued that children have such unshakeable loyalty only for natural parents; but recent research shows that the emotional attachment of adopted children is to their adoptive parents, whether their lives had been particularly happy or not. In one sense adopted children are less at risk because no one adopts by accident. This is an oblique merit of the difficulties and delays: they are a test of loving purpose.

Nor do adoption officers carry their responsibilities alone. The guardian *ad litem* is the court's watch-dog and must make a satisfactory report before an order is made. The guardian's inquiries, as well as the council's investigations, safeguard every third-party adoption to some extent.

I do not believe third parties are 'dangerous' because they are unprofessional. One pair of adopters rejected by a well-known voluntary society wrote to tell me they now had two children through a 'third party' and at no time had it been suggested by the local authority that they were unsuitable people. (As one was a schoolmaster and the other a probation officer, this would be difficult to argue.)

I do not accept that adoption work needs academic profes-sionalism, certainly not the quasi-qualifications which are accepted as suitable training today. Above all, good adoption work demands heart, speed, and resolution. Local councils pride themselves on greater expertise than the voluntary societies but arrange only 3,000 adoptions a year compared with at least 9,500 adoptions by about the same number of voluntary societies, and with some 8,500 third-party adoptions.

If there is official disapproval of third-party adoptions and a sneaking disdain for amateurism within the voluntary societies, why are all local councils not instructed to take on this work? As it is, only about half of the local authorities able to register as adoption agencies have chosen to do so.

The preoccupation with screening of would-be adopters often overlooks that society offers increasing safeguards for all children. District nurses, health visitors, and the school doctors are all on the look-out for signs of trouble in the home. An adopted child should not need greater protection.

The crucial question is—should any potential adopters be refused and if so on what basis? My own views are that adoption agencies should be required to tell adopters why they are turned away and that those who are rejected should have a right of appeal to a family court. This should make agencies reluctant to refuse adopters for specious or flimsy reasons because they would have to be prepared to produce argument and evidence to support their decisions.

Agencies should not be allowed to refuse adopters on the grounds that they have more adopters than children available without providing proof of this fact. The court would have to be convinced that there was not a single child, including those considered difficult to place, older children and the coloured or handicapped, whom this couple could not help.

The excuse that there is no *suitable* child for the couple should always be open to challenge, for 'matching' is a pretentious myth of the adoption world. Adoption is an artificial situation and adopters should not be led to believe otherwise. They ought not to be promised a child 'as alike as possible to the one you might have had yourself'. Who knows what this hypothetical baby would be like anyway?

The popular belief that children are as intelligent as their parents is also highly questionable for it ignores the stimulus of environment and the spur of opportunity. An American study of children adopted in infancy whose mothers were of low social and economic standing (including some who were mentally retarded) showed that they acquired I.Q.s which were average or above. Moreover, the second generation children are now scoring average and above in intelligence tests.

A friend who applied to adopt was asked what his paternal grandfather did. 'I'm not sure,' he said, 'why?' 'We like to match the grandfathers as well as the fathers,' came the fatuous reply. Adopters want a child to love, they are not asking for 'a chip off the old block'.

Undoubtedly, one of the most absurd reasons why there are couples waiting to adopt children who need them is that many adoption proceedings are governed by county boundaries. A number of local authorities will place children only with prospective adopters resident in the council's area; others will accept for placing only children living within their jurisdiction. Some councils make both rules, more than half one of them. The national adoption societies arrange adoptions all over the country but local voluntary societies are territorially restricted. Meanwhile, in Cornwall and Scotland there are not enough adoptive parents. In London the Agnostics Adoption Society is 'flooded with applications', and the Catholic Children's Societies are complaining of ineffective co-operation from local authorities.

The solution lies in an 'adoption resource exchange' which circulates details of children and would-be parents whom agencies cannot help in their own areas. Such an organization has been working successfully in Canada for ten years now. How much longer have we in Britain to wait for the implementation of so simple and useful a scheme?

One reason for reluctance to start a 'resource exchange' may well be that in this country there is common acceptance of the idea that for children for whom it is difficult to find conventionally suitable adopters fostering is a happy second-best. In fact, it provides a makeshift alternative which absolves social workers from making a firm decision, and cloaks the imperative need for more energetic and persuasive efforts to find permanent parents.

Fostering has nothing to commend it for young children except on an emergency basis, because there is no security in the situation and lack of this inevitably undermines worth-while relationships. The foster-child is vulnerable to heartbreaking and accumulative damage. His natural parents may fetch him at any time. The agency which boarded him out may take him away. His foster-parents may send him away because he misbehaves or wets the bed, or shows too little affection.

One suggestion from a conference in Camden is that local councils should be empowered to assume parental rights for any children in their care continuously for three years, or for a total of three years out of five. This has considerable attraction, of course, to those who believe that local councils have the will and the resources to find suitable stable foster-homes where the child is safeguarded from the sudden exercise of parental rights by his natural mother or father. It would, however, only make those homes marginally more secure for the child. This is because it moves authority from the natural parents to the local council and not to the couple looking after the child.

The idea was also put forward at Camden that private foster-parents themselves should have the opportunity to apply for legal custody of a child they have looked after for three years; and, if the child has been five years in their home, the Court could waive the consent of the natural parents to adoption. (It was proposed this should apply to all children who had been five years in one foster home, whether placed privately or by the Council.)

To my mind none of these suggestions are bold enough. As I have proposed earlier, fostering should be tolerated only as a short-term solution and the foster-parents should be prepared after caring for a child for a year to apply for his legal custody or his adoption.

The high failure rate of foster-homes is causing so much alarm that I have heard it said that children's homes may be preferable after all. The argument goes that institutions do at least have

N

skilled and devoted staff and the children know security. The modern Homes are small, more homely and sited in towns rather than in remote country houses.

None of these claims bears much examination. Residential nurseries have stood condemned for more than twenty years by a mass of evidence illustrating their ill-effects. The security they offer is often mythical, for many Homes look after babies only up to the age of five, when those children still without parents are moved. At an age when a child needs special support and affection at home because he is about to start at school, he must leave familiar surroundings for a Home for older children. In the Homes where children may stay until they are ready to stand on their own feet there is no early security either, for the departures of other perhaps more attractive children to new parents are reminders of loneliness and rejection.

The constant change of staff also mocks the claims of most institutions to provide a stable environment. According to the Williams Report, 'Caring for People' (1967), about a third of the staff in all children's Homes leave every year and a lot go because of friction with other members of staff.

The highest turnover of staff is experienced among voluntary homes with fewer than ten children and yet it is generally supposed that these are more stable than larger ones.

So much for the popular image of a motherly woman running a happy cottage-home for a small number of contented children and giving a life-time of devoted service. In truth, the staff, mostly single women, bicker; the children are difficult; and the house-mother leaves for a more highly paid job, or a less onerous one. And when a house-mother quits this is yet another let-down for the deprived child.

Another popular idea is that all modern children's Homes are small. In fact, thirteen children is the average in local authority Homes, and twenty-eight the average in voluntary Homes. Twenty-five per cent of voluntary Homes have more than a hundred children, and those between five and fourteen years are the majority in all Homes. At the time of the Williams inquiry some 1,200 Homes had more than 19,000 children, but this represented only 64 per cent of all children's Homes, those who co-operated in the survey.

The real scale of the tragedy of Britain's 'Home' children in 1967 is almost twice as great—some 35,000 to 40,000 young lives jeopardized by neglect, misfortune, and social services still largely rooted in the concepts of the Victorian age. Nor are the outlines of this picture softened by suggestions that many deprived children are so emotionally disturbed or handicapped that they cannot be considered suitable to live with private families and must rely instead upon skilled remedial care in residential establishments. In most places the skilled care simply is not provided, for 70 per cent of staff in children's Homes are unqualified. Even within specialized homes, such as those for the maladjusted, the proportion of trained staff is only 38 per cent.

There is no requirement that training should be undertaken. Courses of training for the staff of children's Homes have been provided by some voluntary organizations, and, since 1947, by the Central Training Council in Child Care (Home Office). But in eighteen years only about 3,000 students have qualified for the 'Certificate in the Residential Care of Children'. Recently local authorities and voluntary bodies were asked to nominate study supervisors to help plan a new course for residential staff. Such has been the standard of training, however, that the Home Office circular announcing the scheme said these supervisors should have experience and training in the residential care of children *if possible*.

There are nearly 80,000 children in the care of local authorities and voluntary societies (1967) and they are costing the tax-payers more than £32,000,000 a year, to which vast sum must be added the expenditure by voluntary organizations. It is also worth noting that the cost per child per week in a local authority Home is just over £13 (1967).

If things go on as they are in ten years there will be 5,000 more children needing residential care and 1,300 extra staff wanted to look after them. It is wishful thinking to believe that the right people are going to come forward in these numbers and that there will be sufficient money to train them adequately. Moreover, such effort would merely be adding to existing folly. Homes for children are an expensive failure and their continuance in this country is a tragic disgrace and a living monument to ignorance and prejudice.

For generations the public Home has been the symbol of a caring community, a milestone on the painful route of progress from parish relief. Cherished and developed by the Victorians, the Homes have been sustained by a lack of imagination which has all too often confined the idea of charity to the offertory box, the envelope scheme and the broadcast appeal. Much of modern life suffers from a similar humanitarianism without heart. Homes continue to warp the lives of the children they seek to help. It is particularly poignant that children in crisis should be segregated from real family life in environments which threaten to distort their development and to undermine their potential capacities for human happiness. All these Homes hide the results of neglectful parents, failed foster-homes, broken adoptions, and lack of humanity among relations, friends, and neighbours. More homes, more trained staff and an expansion of the whole archaic institutional structure, these are monstrous ideas.

Special homes for special categories of children are a solution to administrators' problems, not the children's. The diabetics, maladjusted, blind, and crippled can be treated as groups; but unless they are ill to a degree beyond parental care they pay a price which is in most cases totally unnecessary and psychologically damaging, removal from loving parents and the normal world.

What is needed is a determined campaign to empty the Homes. This means challenging and accepting the capacity of ordinary people to love children. I believe there is an enormous potential of parents and homes wasted because of prejudiced officials with insufficient faith in the goodness and toughness of human nature.

The needs of all deprived children, healthy and handicapped, must be made known on a national basis, and there should be the most intelligent co-operation between adoption agencies. The true plights of all these children should be made known, emotions stirred and offers of help accepted. I do not believe in the dangers of recruiting the 'wrong people'. Who are all these *wrong* people?

Adoption agencies say that advertisements bring dispropor-
tionately more work than results. Many 'unsatisfactory' people
come forward, aroused only by superficial sentimentality of the
sort which inspires offers to take a child home for Christmas. Of
course some of these applicants might not endure as permanent
parents, but the effect of actually having the child upon their
strength of purpose is never considered.

The crux of the matter remains that elsewhere, and particularly
in America and Canada, far more vigorous efforts are being made
to find parents for all children in crisis. Possibly, in America's
more classless and socially mobile society, adoption is more
acceptable than in a traditionalist society such as ours with its
misplaced emphasis on class and blood lines. Nevertheless, it
should be possible to introduce some of America's energy and
enterprise. In America adoption is quite 'above board' with
adoption ceremonies in churches, adoption weeks, open discussion
forums and extensive publicity. Both America and Canada rightly
attach great importance to the need for community education and
the broadest approach to achieve this.

Ontario is alleged to apply shock tactics not approved by all
sections of public opinion in the placing of children for adoption.
These figures for adoptions in 1965 illustrate the extent to which
use was made of the power to dispense with parental consent:
under one year, 43 per cent; one to three, 26 per cent; four
to six, 9 per cent; seven to fourteen, 14 per cent; and over fourteen years 5 per cent. There has been no follow-up of these older
adopted children, but the breakdown rate during the year's
probation has been very low. In 1964 it was less than 2 per
cent. Child welfare legislation in this part of Canada puts
emphasis in the right place in my opinion: it is made umistak-
ably the duty of workers to place for adoption if at all possible
every child in the wardship of the Crown. (Such wards are
much like the children here for whom the local authority has
assumed parental rights or who have been committed under a
Fit Person Order.) To place a Crown ward for adoption the
Director of Child Welfare must agree but no other consent is
required. This is irrespective of the wishes of the parents although

adoption is only considered if social workers believe that children have no future with their own relatives. The objections which stand in the way of emptying the Homes in Britain are largely due to too many myths, too much patronage, and the false pride of the administrators.

There are thousands of childless homes crying out for children and hundreds of Homes filled with children in need of family life. I do not believe it is impossible to match these needs. There are white healthy babies waiting for adoption. There are children whose parents will neither provide for them nor let them go. Hundreds more are handicapped in finding adopters by age, health, or colour. Even by religion. Many are considered *unsuitable* for adoption, disqualified for love.

In Quebec fourteen years ago the Children's Service Centre was placing children for adoption with congenital heart defects, deafness, and even brain damage, or backgrounds of mental and physical illness. The Open Door Society was formed in Montreal in 1957 to liaise with the Children's Service Centre in promoting and arranging adoptions of non-white children. Now it has agencies across North America which help to place non-white children in white homes, and several organizations similar to the Society have been started. It is customary to board out with a view to adoption children termed 'hard to place'. This may be thought progressive for this country where agencies often say they have not enough adopters of sufficient calibre to take on disabled children and often presume to take the pessimistic view that such children are unacceptable.

Those organizations, like the Crusade of Rescue and Barnardo's, which make real efforts on behalf of these forlorn children are rewarded. The mother of a spina bifida child of six must have moved millions of television viewers when she said in a BBC1 programme on handicapped children (31 October 1967): 'I'd have another one if anybody didn't want one. We'd love to, Faith and I—we've learnt a lot. We have a lot of love and love helps enormously.'

We *need* to advertise unwanted children and to accept more freely those who are prepared to offer them a real home.

Caring about children is not a matter of putting money into envelopes, supporting bazaars, giving the 'Home' children a treat. This is the easy way out, absolving the conscience without personal involvement. Churches of every denomination should play a vigorous part in inspiring their members to adopt, or to foster with a view to adoption or legal custody, and also to show more practical Christianity towards unmarried mothers. Opening their own homes to unmarried mothers and their babies while the mothers make up their minds about adoption would help more than supporting public Homes.

I also think it is high time the religious barriers came down. No child should be denied parents because of the religious stipulations of his mother. After a short time has elapsed her wishes should be put aside entirely in the interests of the child. In a report on racial integration Barnardo's frankly admit that most of their coloured young people brought up in care rejected religion, many because of the 'apparent irrelevance in their circumstances of the Gospel message'.

To find alternative and better solutions for deprived children means wide-scale enrolment of the public. A number of local authorities now provide substitute mothers to keep families together in a crisis. In Birmingham housewives are recruited to take into their own homes motherless families of two, three, or more children, whose fathers will collect them on his way home from work. Children denied home life for a few weeks because of a family emergency—a new baby, a parent's illness—should not be admitted into care. Yet half the children in care are taken over for reasons of this sort. The danger is that the child may be left in the Home long after the emergency is past.

I believe that a guardian *ad litem* should be appointed for every child taken into care, and no such volunteer should have more than six young charges at any one time. The guardian's task would be to ensure that the child is reunited as soon as possible with his family and in the meantime is found a temporary foster-home. If the child is available for adoption the guardian should help to find him parents and supervise boarding out meantime in a foster-home. These guardians must be volunteers divorced from the aura of officialdom which so often surrounds social workers, and children's departments should try to welcome their contribution.

Child care departments are understaffed and the scope of their work grows steadily. In Canada and America there are many examples of volunteers providing emergency housing, befriending unmarried mothers, and teaching household management to problem families. In New York State, Buffalo's emergency parents are on call throughout the night when the children's welfare office is closed.

People who volunteer to empty the children's Homes should be helped up to the hilt, and one effective way would be to deploy the staff made redundant in private homes. A Home and a training establishment are incompatible so let the nursery nurses become part of the Children's Department and be sent where they are most needed, to hard-pressed foster- or adoptive-mothers, to families in difficulties, or to unmarried mothers not yet able to manage on their own.

If the institutional Homes were closed large resources of money and people could be channelled into real homes. Disinherited children are a tragic waste. A dynamic force of professionals and volunteers could combine to provide Britain with the most enlightened and effective Child Rescue Service in the world, one in which no child need ever be confined within a private world of loneliness and bitterness.

Appendix

1. FOSTERING RATES 1968

Boarding-out payments are fixed independently by local authorities and vary from one area to another. Voluntary societies do not operate a standard scale either so I offer here as a sample the fostering rates of a London borough, a county council with a large rural population, and one of the well-known voluntary societies.

Special allowances may be paid where fostering presents special problems. It is difficult to be specific but a number of London boroughs authorize a special rate 'for children receiving specially skilled care' of up to £1 a day, and up to £2 a day 'for older boys and girls presenting acute problems'. Voluntary societies do make special payments for certain children, such as bed-wetters, but do not on the whole offer substantial bonuses.

2. LONDON BOROUGH OF HAMMERSMITH

Age (years)	Maintenance per week s. d.	Clothing per week s. d.	Pocket Money per week s. d.	Total per week s. d.
0–2	38 6	9 6	1 0	49 0
3–4	42 0	9 6	1 0	52 6
5–6	42 0	12 3	1 9	56 0
7–8	44 6	12 6	2 6	59 6
9	45 6	14 0	3 6	63 0
10	48 6	14 0	4 0	66 6
11	50 0	15 6	4 6	70 0
12	52 6	16 0	5 0	73 6
13	53 0	17 6	6 6	77 0
14	58 0	19 0	7 0	84 0
At School { 15	59 6	21 0	14 0	94 6*
16	59 6	24 6	17 6	101 6*
17	63 0	24 6	21 0	108 6*

3. COUNTY OF DEVON

Age (years)	Maintenance per week s. d.	Pocket Money per week s. d.	Total per week s. d.	Clothing per quarter s. d.
Under 5	42 0	7	42 7	117 0
5 and 6	45 6	1 2	46 8	136 6
7	45 6	1 9	47 3	136 6
8	49 0	2 4	51 4	149 6
9 and 10	49 0	2 11	51 11	149 6
11	52 6	3 6	56 0	169 0
12	52 6	4 1	56 7	169 0
13	56 0	4 8	60 8	195 0
14	56 0	5 10	61 10	195 0
15	63 0	10 6	73 6	208 0
16 (at school)	63 0	12 10	75 10	208 0

* Plus cost of school dinners in term time.

4. DR. BARNARDO'S

Age (years)	Maintenance per week s. d.	Clothing per week s. d.	Pocket Money per week s. d.	Total per week s. d.
0–4	32 6	8 6	9	41 9
5	35 6	10 0	1 3	46 9
6	35 6	10 0	1 6	47 0
7	35 6	10 0	1 9	47 3
8	38 6	11 6	2 0	52 0
9	38 6	11 6	2 3	52 3
10	38 6	11 6	2 6	52 6
11	42 0	13 0	2 9	57 9
12	42 0	13 0	3 6	58 6
13	45 6	14 0	6 0	65 6
14	45 6	14 0	8 0	67 6
15	50 0	15 0	10 0	75 0
16	52 6	15 0	12 6	80 0
17	55 0	17 6	12 6	85 0

Acknowledgements

It is not always easy to explain complicated procedures from first principles. Invariably, it takes much time. Many of those engaged in welfare work among unmarried parents have given freely from their knowledge and experience of one of the most intractable areas of human grief. I am grateful to them. Also I am particularly indebted to those would-be adopters who wrote from the depths of their private miseries in the hope that my work might stimulate reforms which would lead to more homeless children finding loving parents.

Index

55/816

12/62